AYATULLAH IBRAHIM AMINI

Resurrection (Qiyamah) in the Qur'an

First published by Ansariyan Publications 2011

Copyright © 2011 by Ayatullah Ibrahim Amini

All rights reserved. No part of this publication may be reproduced, stored or transmitted in any form or by any means, electronic, mechanical, photocopying, recording, scanning, or otherwise without written permission from the publisher. It is illegal to copy this book, post it to a website, or distribute it by any other means without permission.

First edition

Translation by Sayyid Athar Husain S. H. Rizvi

Contents

Introduction	1
Evidences of resurrection	5
Soul in the Quran	27
Death and its hardships	34
In the Grave	42
Purgatory (Barzakh)	50
Signs of the Judgment Day	73
Judgment Day in Quran	81
Gathering of humans (Hashr)	86
Scroll of deeds	90
Scale of deeds	97
Accounting of deeds	104
Intercession (Shafa'ah)	121
Siraat Bridge	134
Hell	141
Paradise and its bounties	152
Bibliography	164
Epilogue	165

Introduction

Where do I go after death? Would I return once again? What was the aim of my creation? Is it necessary to ponder upon these points? What is imminent would definitely come to pass; so why to worry about it? Imagination of death and the events after it make ones life disagreeable, so why should I worry about it and lose sleep over it?

Yes, these questions arose throughout the ages and occupied the minds of people in the past and still do so; and are on the verge of getting convincing replies. Therefore intellectuals and philosophers tried to answer these questions to realize the truth; satisfy themselves and that they may hand over the conclusions of their researches to others.

Divine messengers believed in resurrection and based the foundation of their call on it. In heavenly religions, life after death is considered a necessary principle of faith and hundreds and thousands of books are written in different languages on this subject. The Messenger of Allah (s) and the Holy Imams ('a) hold a very eminent position in propagating and proving faith in resurrection. The Holy Quran has stressed on this matter more than other heavenly scriptures, and has explained its various aspects in many verses. Deep contemplation on the verses of this heavenly Book, along with their interpretation through the sayings of the Messenger of Allah (s) and the Holy Imams ('a) can enable us to understand life after death, which is an unseen world; as without that it would have been impossible for us to do so. That is why we have based this book on verses of Quran; with the hope that it would be useful for all those who are in search of truth and especially that it may benefit the youth.

Before actual discussion, we think that it is necessary to mention some features about the two convergent views on resurrection: the view of believers and the view of disbelievers.

Life, according to the two views

Faith in resurrection sometimes does not go beyond the limit of words and imagination, as it is not actual faith and does not have the qualities of the world and the hereafter and sometimes it goes beyond the stage of meaning and reaches to genuine faith. This is in fact true faith in resurrection and it will have the traces of the world and the hereafter with it according to the resolution of the person in carrying out the duties made incumbent on him and depending on the strength of his faith.

Views of the believers about resurrection

Those who have real faith in resurrection do not consider their lives limited to a few years in this world; on the contrary, they have a broad view and they know that it is only a beginning; and that it is going to continue forever in the hereafter.

They don't regard death as annihilation and the end of life; on the contrary they consider it to be a means of being transferred to the world of the hereafter and an eternal life in that world. They consider themselves to be travelers, who have come into this world to equip

Introduction

themselves for the perpetual life of the hereafter. Such persons, just as they follow a detailed plan and make efforts in this limited life of the world, in the same way they are also not unmindful of their life in the hereafter. They consider the world to be a harvest field for the hereafter and consider their lives to be the best provision of obtaining the means of building a prosperous after life. They do not waste the most valuable capital in useless ways, lest they should face regret on the day of resurrection. They know this and they believe in the sayings of the prophets that man is a being having a free will and is answerable for his good and bad deeds in the hereafter. His success and misfortune in the hereafter will depend on his beliefs and morals in this world. Paradise and the bounties of Paradise and Hell and the chastisements of Hell in the hereafter will be based on his good or bad deeds in this world. Such a person would be aware of his duties, have a good nature, is a well wisher, trustworthy, truthful and justice loving. And he will avoid bad morals and evil deeds. In face of the calamities of the world and difficulties of life, which are there for everyone, whether one likes them or not, he does not evade and does not protest; on the contrary he remains absolutely patient and says: Indeed we belong to Allah and to Him we shall return.

During old age and the last period of his life, he does not abandon patience and hope; and he is not afraid of death as he has the good news of the future and he knows where he is going.

In this condition, faith in resurrection does not impel man to go into isolation and give up social duties; on the contrary it prepares him to obtain knowledge, and to discover the secrets of nature, his life, population of the world, social service, defense of human values and martyrdom; since it is with faith in resurrection and rewards of the hereafter that sacrificing ones life in the path of truth can be justified. How peaceful and pleasing is life in the shade of belief in resurrection! Alas, if all the people had faith in hereafter and accounting of deeds!

What is the beauty in such a supposed world?

But what is the life of the deniers of resurrection like? It is very short and death means the end of life and decline into the valley of non-existence. For them, life in this world is regrettably full of sorrow and grief; it is futile and aimless and without logical justification. During calamities, the denier of resurrection is discouraged by difficulties of life that befall everyone intentionally or unintentionally and he is not comfortable in them. And any sort of pleading is also not effective. Sometimes, in order to comfort his inward pains, he resorts to alcoholic drinks and other drugs, so that he may for sometime forget himself and his painful thoughts. But temporary intoxication is also of no use. Sometimes he is so much affected by the severity of discomfort and feelings of discouragements that he commits suicide. When a denier of resurrection witnesses injustice of oppressors on himself or others, and their successful escape from legal punishments, he becomes despondent and is convinced that there is no justice in this world and no sort of reward and punishment. Denial of resurrection necessitates that practicing good morals, doing good to others, defending the rights of the deprived, sacrifice and martyrdom in defense of truth etc. should not have rational justification and practical cover. The most difficult period of the life of a denier in resurrection is when he is down with an incurable disease or extreme old age when he knows that death is imminent; at that time he despairs of life and can only imagine himself falling into a deep oblivion of nothingness. Alas! How terrifying is the imagination of annihilation into nothingness and inexistence! How difficult and unbearable is life without faith in resurrection! The cause of most oppressions, battles, and violation of rights, killings and murders, crimes, cruelties, corruptions is denial in resurrection. If all the people of the world become deniers in resurrection, accounting, rewards and punishments; what a terrible world it would be!

Evidences of resurrection

Resurrection is one of the important and difficult problems of philosophy and scholasticism. In books of scholastic theology, it is discussed in detail and hundreds of books are written on this subject. Since the books of this present series are supposed to be compact and simple, we would try to prove this belief through basic arguments that may be clearly understood by all:

1- **Nature**

Nature is in the meaning of a special creation. Innate features are matters of natural characteristics embedded in the nature of human beings, which arise from the conscience of every perfect human being and do not need reasoning and evidence. Attention to conscience and waking up of nature to accept them is sufficient. Recognition of beauty is natural. Every sane and mature person can understand beauty. He considers some things to be beautiful and some he finds lacking in beauty. All are having this nature, although it is possible that there might be difference in their applications and manner. The goodness of equitability, truthfulness and the evil of injustice and falsehood and betrayal of truth are also like this. The origin of attention to God, humility to Him and His worship are also natural matters present in the being of every human. Awakening of the nature in faith in them is sufficient, although it is possible that some persons would commit a mistake in recognition of its aims and get deviated; such as the origin of idol worship, which came into being in this way.

Misunderstanding of idolaters and followers of nonsense lies in the fact that in specifying the applicability or sense of God, about which the innate nature testifies, they fell into an illusion and in ignorance went into deviation.

Desire for perpetuity and life after death is also an established matter and is present in the innate being of every man and from that springs the God-given source and it shows its effects; even though throughout history and in some communities and sects, they are mixed with a number of nonsensical matters.

2- History

All this leads us to conclude that belief in the perpetuity of human soul and life after death is deeply rooted in human history and even in pre-historic man and communities that are now extinct.

So much so, that history and excavations of ancient graveyards show and archeological studies like the pyramids of Egypt and other communities and nations, which have come down to us that most people of the past had belief in perpetuity of soul and life after death. Therefore they buried their dead with their personal effects, belongings and things, which they might need; continued to perform rituals to honor the dead for a long period of time and sending offerings and charities on their behalf.

Regarding this, Will Durant says:

Since Sumerians (524 B.C.) buried with their dead, provisions and objects of their use, we can conclude that they had belief in life after death.[1]

He also writes:

The body, Egyptians believed, was inhabited by a small replica of itself called the 'ka', and also by a soul that dwelt in the body like a bird flitting among trees. All of these: body, ka and soul – survived the appearance of death; they could escape mortality for a time in proportion as the flesh was preserved from decay; but if they came to Osiris clean of all sin they would be permitted to live forever in the "Happy Field of Food" – those heavenly gardens where there would always be abundance and security.[2]

Then he writes:

The Mycenaean himself, as well as most of his art, is found in the tombs; for he folded and buried his dead in uncomfortable jars, and seldom cremated them as the Heroic Age would do. Apparently he believed in a future life, for many objects of use and value were placed in the graves.[3]

He further writes:

According to Egyptian belief, these Elysian Fields, however, could be reached only through the services of a ferryman, an Egyptian prototype of Charon; and this old gentleman would receive into his boat only such men and women as had done no evil in their lives. Or Osiris would question the dead, weighing each candidate's heart in the scale against a feather to test his truthfulness. Those who failed in this final examination would be condemned to lie forever in their tombs, hungering and thirsting, fed upon by hideous crocodiles, and never coming forth to see the sun.[4]

---

[1] Story of Civilization, Vol. 1, Pg. 155
[2] Story of Civilization, Vol. 1, Pg. 241
[3] Story of Civilization, Vol. 2, Pg. 49
[4] Story of Civilization, Vol. 1, Pg. 241

From what is stated above and from hundreds of other examples, we can conclude that belief in life after death is an ancient phenomenon present in the innate nature of man, in such a way that the ancient man even through his simple understanding was able to obtain and have faith in it. Although priests and temple assistants had role in promoting this belief and in order to misuse it, invented nonsense and rumors, but the actual belief in life after death was not their creation; on the contrary they took advantage of the belief present in the innate nature of man. Will Durant writes in this regard as follows:

The priest did not create religion, he merely used it, as a statesman uses the impulses and customs of mankind; religion arises not out of sacerdotal invention or chicanery, but out of the persistent wonder, fear, insecurity, hopefulness and loneliness of men.[5]

Although prophets throughout the history of whom Prophet Adam ('a) was the first; and who is also called as the father of humanity had a role in formation of belief in God and life after death, but they did not invent this belief; on the contrary they only tried to awaken the innate nature of man, to strengthen the beliefs and to purify and train the self. And since their call was based on innate nature they also had divine support.

Therefore it can be said: Since belief in resurrection existed throughout the ages in the nature of human beings, it can be counted as an innate and original belief. It should also be mentioned that we don't claim that all human beings in all the ages had belief in life after death and acted according to it. On the contrary, throughout the ages and even today there are persons who because of ignorance, rebellion and selfish desires suppress their human nature in their acts; sometimes they almost deny resurrection verbally. As attributed to Assyrians and ancient Babylonians that they had no faith in resurrection, heaven or

---

[5] Story of Civilization, Vol. 1, Pg. 83

hell.[6]

But this type of doubts even leading to verbal denial is natural and it does not harm faith in resurrection in any way. Deniers of resurrection have no evidence to support their claim. On the contrary since their reality had not become clear to them and the selfish desires overcame them, they denied resurrection till they became free from following the base desires. And in the terminology it can be said that they preferred immediate joy instead of the promise of future enjoyments.

Will Durant has quoted the statement of a denier of resurrection as follows:

Saddest of all is a poem engraved upon a slab now in the Leyden Museum, and dating back to 2200 B.C. Carpe diem, it sings: None cometh from thence. That he may tell us how they fare; that we may content our hearts; until we too depart to the place whither they have gone.[7]

Will Durant has presented the above statement in his book as an evidence of denial of resurrection while the fact is that it does not at all show any such denial; on the contrary the opening lines say that no one has returned from that side to explain its existence to us; he has expressed doubt about it and has preferred immediate pleasure to the promise of Paradise and said that he wanted instant happiness. Today also we see most deniers of resurrection using the same argumentation.

3- Desire for Perpetuity

One of the signs of nature is to desire perpetuity and inclination to live forever. Man always makes efforts to continue to live as long as possible. And since he knows that his death is imminent, he tries to leave

---

[6] Story of Civilization, Vol. 1, Pg. 283

[7] Story of Civilization, Vol. 1, Pg. 234

behind his influence. He trains his children, writes books, performs acts of charity, and makes bequests with regard to commemoration assemblies and offerings at the place of his burial. He wants his plans and aspirations to endure forever and sometimes he even gives up his life to defend them. All these are signs of a desire for perpetuity and eternality. If he considered death as the end of his life and annihilation, what will be the use of commemoration assemblies, presence of children and a respectable place of burial? If he has faith in death of annihilation, how will he justify sacrificing his life for the defense of his views and aims. All this leads us to conclude that desire to live forever after the death is present in the being of every man and it is a natural factor. These natural desires must be beyond investigation and if not, the presence of such desires in man would be meaningless and none of the actions of the all-knowing and wise God is meaningless.

4- Immortality

In the discussion of knowing God, it was proved that the wide world is having the being of God, who is the creator and controller of the creatures. His knowledge, power and wisdom were also proved and also that He never does anything illogical and aimless. But His aim in the creation of the world was not to satisfy any of His needs since He is needless; on the contrary His aim was to benefit and perfect. He bestows perfection to every phenomenon according to its capability. His gracefulness is in His being and miserliness is not present therein. Between the phenomena of the world, man is having an extraordinary and a distinctive position in his capability.

His body is from the material world and his soul is from the spiritual and the celestial world. The material world, throughout years and extremely long centuries, has developed the capacity through perfections of actions and reactions so that it may assume the form of an astounding man. His physical constitution is composed of digestive system, organs of hearing, sight, smell, speech, reproduction, blood circulation and other organs, which operate through astonishing niceties, some of which are mentioned in books of science.

More important than all this is especially the creation of the celestial soul of man; his reasoning power and intelligence; and an extraordinary mechanism of his thinking faculty consisting of his learning ability and memory retention. Man is created in such a way that he is able to remove the curtain from the secrets of the world through contemplation, reasoning and his experience and controls the material world one after another. He inhabits the world and makes it useful for himself and other human beings. Therefore, all the phenomena of the material world, different types of plants and animal, earth, mines, atmosphere, light and elements are practically at the disposal of man and he has the power to control and use them at present or in the future.

In conclusion, we can define man as the by-product of rotation and search of the material world and the pick of the whole lot of the system of creation. Aim of creation of the world should also be searched in him.

Now this important question arises that can we consider that the aim of creation of this world and most important of all, creation of man whose life is at the most a hundred years, which is filled with various types of hardships, calamities and unhappiness is short in comparison to the seeking of pleasures and to say: Death is the end of life of man and his complete annihilation? Your reply is an absolutely negative. If it was so, creation and running of the material world; its coming into existence and life of man would all have been meaningless. An absurd action is not expected from any sane person; how can we expect it from the Almighty Allah, who is all-powerful, all-knowing, wise and needless?

Therefore it can be said that man is created for an everlasting life in the hereafter and not for destruction and annihilation. The aim of the Almighty Allah in creation of man is that he should live in this world and train himself in good manners and good deeds and prepare for an everlasting good life in the hereafter. He created him with this aim, equipped him with ability for perfection programmed for his personal success of the hereafter. He also sent prophets to guide man. In this way, creation of world and man can be justified rationally.

This is indicated in the verses of Quran; as for example:

"And We did not create the heaven and the earth and what is between them for sport."(21:16)

"What! did you then think that We had created you in vain and that you shall not be returned to Us?" (23:115)

"And We did not create the heavens and the earth and what is between them two but in truth; and the hour is most surely coming..."(15:85)

5- Reward and punishment

In the discussion about the cognition of God, it was proved that the Almighty Allah is just and the creation of man and the world was based on justice. He bestows perfection to everything according to its capacity and does not allow the right of any phenomenon or man to be violated. Since injustice is due to ignorance or needfulness of one who commits it and the creator of the world is pure from every defect.

Injustice is an evil deed, and the Almighty Allah never commits an evil deed. Not only the Almighty Allah does not commit injustice, on the contrary He also desires to be kind and just to man. And He has not allowed them to act unjustly with each other. In the Holy Quran He says:

"Surely Allah enjoins the doing of justice and the doing of good (to others) and the giving to the kindred, and He forbids indecency and evil and rebellion; He admonishes you that you may be mindful." (16:90)

The Almighty Allah has fixed laws and duties for the purification of the life of man, which is surrounded by injustice and oppression, so that he may lead a life of peace and success. And through the messenger prophets and His selected representatives they should be kind to each other and keep away from injustice and sins. He has fixed good rewards for the doers of good, and decreed severe punishments for oppressors and sinners. But regrettably all people are not same with regard to social duties; they are of two types: one is group of those who are aware of their duties, well wisher and righteous; they neither oppress others and nor cause harm to anyone. On the contrary, they are seekers of justice for those whose rights have been violated and those who have been oppressed. So much so that those who tread this path have to face deprivations, are subjected to imprisonments and cast themselves into dangers. They are good natured, trustworthy, truthful, having a good character, helpful and who are cognizant of truth. Another group is of those who live in such a way in this world, but they are not rewarded for their good deeds in the world. And sometimes, as a result of their good behavior, they even have to face deprivation and numerous hardships. As a result of truthfulness and seeking justice they are subjected to torture and imprisonment at the hands of tyrants and oppressors and sometimes they sacrifice their lives. Should there not be another world where the doers of good receive rewards for their good deeds. If the hereafter and good rewards had not been there, would it have been according to the justice of the Almighty Allah?

If earth is the end of life, what will be the rational justification of righteousness and piety and holy war (Jihad) and martyrdom on the path of seeking justice?

Another group is that of oppressors; who have no qualms in causing harm to others and in violating the rights of people. They are power hungry, tyrannical and greedy. They prefer their own good and the good of those who are related to them over the good of others. They do not refrain from any injustice in order to gain power and wealth. They subject their opponents to prison and torture and even eliminate them: they usurp their properties and do not refrain from any crime. Not only individuals, they even eliminate communities and nations through imperialism and dictatorship. They have no qualms about committing even the most shameless crimes. On the contrary, they enjoy it and exalt themselves. Such criminals were numerous throughout history and are still present in the world. Although some of them received some punishment in this world, but it was definitely less than the crime that they committed, but most of them did not receive any punishment for their crimes.

The righteous and sinners will be rewarded and punished according to their good deeds and crimes after a short while. Should not there be a world, where each of them is exactly accounted for with regard to his or her deeds? And that the doers of good receive his or her rewards and the sinners are punished in accordance to their crimes? If the world of the hereafter had not been there, what would have been the rational justification of the creation of this world, which is full of injustice and crime? Is this compatible with divine justice? If there is no other world of reward and punishment, why God has commanded observing justice and refraining from injustice? What is the decision of your intellects with regard to this? All would definitely reply: The righteous and sinners are not equal. There is another world after this world, in which the deeds of people will be verified. The righteous will be given a good recompense and sinners will be awarded a severe punishment. The same thing is implied in the verses of the Holy Quran:

"Shall We treat those who believe and do good like the mischief-makers in the earth? Or shall We make those who guard (against evil) like the wicked?" (38:28)

"Nay! do those who have wrought evil deeds think that We will make them like those who believe and do good that their life and their death shall be equal? Evil it is that they judge. And Allah created the heavens and the earth with truth and that every soul may be rewarded for what it has earned and they shall not be wronged." (45:21-22)

6- Abstract nature of the soul

To prove the perpetuity of the soul of man and life after death we can reason through various justifications and one of them is through abstraction of human soul. The abstract nature of human self is a difficult philosophical problem. This important matter is studied in detail in books of philosophy like: Asfar, Risala Tasawwur wa Tasdeeq and other books of Mulla Sadra as well as in the commentary on Zaadul Musafir and Isharaat of Abu Ali Sina and Sharh Manzuma of Mulla Hadi Sabzawari. In this brief writing, we cannot explain this matter in detail, but we shall discuss some evidences of the same. Before the actual discussion, it is necessary to mention some points in brief:

Meaning of Abstractness

Existent beings are of two types: material and abstract. Material beings are as follows: non-living things like stone, dust, different kinds of minerals, metals, chemicals, pigments, water etc; in this category are included gases, energy and even rays of light are considered material things and in the same way, plants and animals also fall into this category as they are also supposed to have souls called animal soul. Material things possess the following qualities: quantity, space, time, movement, change, remoteness and proximity, survival and decay. Such factors are the signs of the material existing beings. Material matters can be perceived through one of the senses or their presence can be discovered through experimentation. The second type is the abstract things: like God; angels are supernatural beings and they do not possess qualities of material beings like place, time, quantity, movement, change, survival and decay. To be abstract is to mean lacking in material qualities.

Definition of the self

Some existing things have souls like the different plants, which possess vegetative souls. Living things like animals are in possession of animal spirits and human beings possess human souls. With regard to plants, it is said: even though their bodies are composed of various elements like water, air, minerals, chemicals, energy, different metals, compounds etc. and they do not possess a soul. But with regard to the fact that this new compound possesses new qualities like: nutrition, maturity and birth etc. thus it would be said: the source of these effects is the vegetative soul, which came into being through compounding of these elements. Especially with regard to animals it can also be said: Although their body is composed of various elements like: water, air, matter, chemicals, energy, various metals etc, but since in this combination new qualities like perception, voluntary movement have come into existence, it is said that the origin of these new qualities lies in the animal soul.

Especially man also can be said to have the same qualities, since he possesses the qualities of self-awareness, perception and senses, memory: hence it can be said: the origin of these new qualities is the human soul.

Through these explanations we realize the reality of the soul. Here we consider it necessary to mention that man is multi-dimensional. On one side his body is a compound of different natural elements and the effect of each of them is present in him. On the other hand, he is a named body, capable of nutrition, maturity and reproduction and he also possesses a vegetative soul. On the other hand, he is an animal possessing an animal soul and having animal instincts.

Finally, a man is a conscious human soul possessing distinctive qualities. It is said that although the vegetative, animal and human souls have come together in man, each of them is having a separate identity and are considered to be the various stages of his existence. The organizing human body is the single human soul, which performs different actions in different stages. The soul and intellect of man is the controller of the human body, and it should control different actions of the vegetative and animal soul in different stages and should persuade them according to actual exigencies.

Evidences of the abstractness of the soul

Among the distinctive qualities of man, which makes him superior to all creatures is the quality of knowledge. Knowledge means awareness, understanding and cognition. Every conscience can understand that some things possess awareness. Evidence of this is not needful of reasoning. Sadruddin Shirazi says: Knowledge can be defined as the presence of form of existing things in view of intellect. Knowledge by nature is determined and revealed and know-how is revealed through knowledge.[8]

With regard to knowledge, it is necessary to know that one should be in the presence of the scholar. This presence is only possible when the knower and the known thing is material. Since if both or one of them is material, they would be unseen by the other and not possible to be exposed or become present. Hence to prove the abstract nature of the soul of man, it is necessary to undertake a deep study about the kinds of knowledges and their kinds.

In books of philosophy, knowledge is divided into two types: present and obtainable. Sadruddin Shirazi has written in this regard that knowledge with the present reality; sometimes the existence of his knowledge is the very same knowledge seen by him, like the knowledge of abstract with his own being and like knowledge of self with regard to his own self and qualities depending on the self and his own actions and spiritual phenomena.

Such knowledges are named as innate knowledges. Also sometimes the presence of knowledge is without the presence of identical existence like our knowledge of things, which are beyond our being and perceptive powers; like earth, man and horse etc. which are named as acquired and affective knowledges.[9] We shall explain both of them here in more detail:

Innate Knowledge

As mentioned previously, knowledge of the self is itself innate knowl-

---

[8] Risala Tasawwur wa Tasdeeq, Pg. 307

[9] Risala Tasawwur wa Tasdeeq, Pg. 307

edge; that is the self of man possesses an awareness and understanding of its own being. He considers himself to be an individual and a separate being and keeps this in mind always and is never ignorant of it. He can forget everything; but he never forgets his ego. He considers himself to be an individual possessing a separate self throughout his brief lifespan. This 'I' through the passage of time and changes of times does not undergo any change even though all these factors have profound effect on his body etc. This 'I' is not hands, feet, eyes, ears, tongue, brain or heart etc. On the contrary, all of them are connected with him. Although according to testimony of intellectuals all parts of body are in constant change throughout the life, and they are changed tens of times, this 'I' is always stable and permanent, with the supposition that even though he may lose or change his organs and limbs, he can never be divested of his identity and it would be same as it was before. Therefore, it must be remembered that the ego of man, which we refer to as 'I' is not material and changeable; on the contrary it is an abstract thing. Since the abstract is from the material and effects of matter, it is always exposed to itself, and it is having innate knowledge about itself; that is the personality and reality of its self is determined and known to itself and is not unseen from it. In other words, knowledge, the knower and the known are one and the same.

This shows that in order to prove the self there is no need to reason from its actions and effects; because Decarates has reasoned from this way and said: "I think therefore I am". On the contrary, before reasoning through thinking, one should be aware of oneself so that one is able to reason out ones action. If one has no awareness of his own self, one cannot reason through ones action, which is its effect.

We quote the statement of Abu Ali Sina to support and explain further the innate knowledge of man with regard to his self[10]:

---

[10] Al-Isharaat wa Tanbihaat, Part 2

He addresses himself: Imagine yourself in each of these four conditions:

First condition: In sanity and perfect physical health: In this condition you will find your self as a person about whom you are well aware; and you will not become unmindful of him in any way.

Second condition: While you are asleep: In this condition, your conscious senses are suspended and you do not feel your body or external things; but you are not unaware of your self, which you call as 'I'. (If someone calls you, you wake up and reply to him).

Third condition: Intoxication (senselessness). In this condition your outward and inward perceptions are suspended and you don't feel anything; but even in that condition your awareness about yourself is intact.

Fourth condition: Just suppose you are created all of a sudden with sanity and perfect physical health in a vaccum and you are not under any kind of pressure that you should be aware of your body. In this condition also, you would not be oblivious of your self; you would be aware of yourself.

Therefore, there is no doubt that man understands his self in every condition. In this way, we have one who understands and a thing which is understood. Now let us see what is understood and who has understood it?

In order to understand the two, the Shaykh employs the realization addressed to his self, and says: Ponder well whether you can perceive yourself with outward senses or through intellect and inward faculties? It is well known that outward and inward faculties have no role in this; since you were unaware of them in the mentioned supposition. Thus they are not the ones who perceive, on the contrary your intellect directly, and the body through senses, are the perceiving ones.

Now let us see what is the perceived (Mudrik)? What is that, which you call "I"?

Is it the apparent aspect of the body, which is visible to the eyes and which can be perceived through the sense of touch? Or with a little concentration you can understand that you are not organs and skin of the body, because you do not change with their change and transformation, on the contrary you are the same person as before. Moreover, as stated before, it is possible for you to become oblivious of them, but you can never become oblivious of your own self.

You are also not like internal organs as the heart, nerves and brain etc. because they cannot be perceived even with outward and inner senses and their proof is needful of anatomical dissection.

This clearly shows that you (the perceived one) are neither the outward nor inward organs of the body; on the contrary you are something, which cannot be perceived and which does not possess the signs of perceptible things.

At that moment the Shaykh mentions to himself the doubts and then replies to them. He says: Perhaps you may say: I prove my existence with my own action, which is the effect of itself (as Descartes has said: I think therefore I am). Then he replies that objection in two ways:

First reply: In such a supposition, you should pay attention to your act, so that you may be able to prove your self through it. Whereas it was stated before that without paying attention to anything, even your own action, you can perceive your self.

Second reply: If you want, you can prove your own self through presence of absolute action; but it is not right since presence of absolute action proves the undetermined doer and not a particular personality (self) and if you want to prove a particular act, which was committed by you, to reason out your existence; it is also incorrect. Because in this supposition it is necessary that you should identify your being as the cause of this act or at least consider it to be contemporary to it, so that you can prove your own being through it.

In that case, before reasoning you had awareness of your own being and reasoning through the act is meaningless. In any case, reasoning through presence of act to prove the doer is not valid reasoning.

The following important points can be derived from the statements of the Shaykh:

- Man is always, at every moment and in every condition, aware of his self.
- This perception is direct and without any medium.
- In this perception, the one who perceives and that which is perceived, are both not from material and perceptive things.
- In this perception, the knower and the known is one reality, and not more and that is the definition of the self of man.
- In this perception, the reality of the known is having presence and exposition for the knower of the reality; that is it is innate knowledge and not acquired through the mind.
- The self of man is a non-perceptible and non-material thing.
- Since it is abstract and free of matter and material effects, corruption has no access to it and it will be everlasting.

Acquired Knowledge

Now that we have learnt what innate knowledge is and that it consists of the presence of self, which is known to the knower. In this instance, the knower perceived the known directly and without any intermediary. Now let us see what acquired knowledge is. In this case, the knower becomes aware of a thing through external form and sense, which that thing has acquired. The thing known to a person in this case is in the beginning and by nature a mental form and when the mental form develops an aspect of exposure by external phenomenon, through this it perceives external phenomenon. Thus in acquired knowledge, a medium called form or sense is present between the knower and the known.

Mental forms can be of two kinds: Partial and general.

Partial forms are concepts which only denote a particular person and are not applicable to more than one person like the mental sense of Muhammad, Hasan, Husain, Fatima… etc. The sense of Muhammad that we have in our mind is only of one single person and it alone cannot imply a number of people. Partial mental forms can also be of two types:

A) Perceptions: The knowledge of man obtained through one of the apparent senses, like sight, hearing, smell, taste and touch. When man through one of these five senses establishes contact with an external phenomenon; and after the action and reaction that comes into being between these two, he comes to know about that external phenomenon. This knowledge will last only as long as the contact is on. After it is off, the connection of awareness is also discontinued.

B) Memories: The contact that man retains through one of the senses with external phenomena leaves an imprint on his being, which remains even when the contact is discontinued. If this effect is from perceptible things, it would be stored in the faculty known as thought or memory. Whenever he likes, he may refer to the archives and recall that previous form and make use of it.

And if the mentioned effect is from partial meaning, it is stored in archives of the faculty called imagination. Like love or hatred perceived between two persons, or fear or attachment, especially which one develops with a person or thing. Such concepts are stored in the faculty of imagination and may be recalled at time of need.

General senses and forms: A general sense can be defined as a mental form, which describes a common aspect of numerous persons and it is applicable to each of them. Like the connotation of 'human being', which can be applied to each of them separately. It can be said: Muhammad is a human being, Ali is a human being, Hameed is a human being and Ashraf is a human being…and so on. And same is the case of terms like animal, substance, vegetation and their parts. Such types of general senses that in the external aspect have an external application are called primary rationalities. We have another general type, which are called philosophical rationalities. They are senses, which do not have an absolute outward implication; on the contrary, human mind through making an analogy between two external phenomena makes an abstraction of these senses. General sense of cause and effect is of this type; for example, we consider external fire as the cause of burning and burning cotton as its effect and we say: fire is the cause and burning cotton is the effect. But causation is not an additional quality of fire. It is not that externally we can have a fire and the quality of causation. On the contrary it is human intellect that can derive causality and effectivity through comparison between fire and burning cotton. Causality in the outward is having reality, but it is the manner of existence of fire and not an added quality.

From this discussion it becomes clear that we have two kinds of general rationalities: primary rationalities and philosophical rationalities.

Now the question arises that through which medium are the generalities perceived and who is their perceiver?

Is it possible to perceive and recognize them through the five senses, brain and nerves?

In reply it is said: Since the absolute natures like man, animal, tree, stone do not have an external existence by the quality of generality, they cannot be perceived through the five senses. That which is present in the outward is the person of man and not the man generally. Implications of man, like: Hasan, Husain and…can be perceived through senses, but the absolute man does not exist with the quality of generality outwardly that he could be perceived through senses. Connotations produced in the mind from each individual person only describe this and can only implied as such (as an individual). In such a case we also have the connotation of man in our mind, which is common to all human beings and which can be applied to each of them separately. Therefore it can be said: The general perceptive man is not but the soul and intellect without the mediums of senses. It is intellect that perceives the quantum of commonality between persons of different natures and constructs the general human being along with the fact that the five senses have no interference in making sense. It should be said: An act is abstract and non-material. This proves that the doer of this act, the self, also be an abstract and non-material reality since it is not possible for a material doer to perform an abstract function. Therefore it should be said: Rising of absolute senses to the self of man is an originative rising and not transmigrative or reactionary.

Now another important question arises: what is the abode of memory and where are the forms and meanings stored? Does the brain or nerves play the role of archives?

Its reply is that since brain and nerves are material, they cannot serve as safe repositories of intellectual forms and connotations, because as intellectual have said, all the parts of the body, like brain and nerves, as a result of nutrition and growth are constantly changing and are being renewed. Physical parts of the body of man are completely changed a number of times during his lifetime. If the location of memory had been the brain and nerves, the forms and meanings stored in them would also be changed along with the change of these organs after a period of time. But such a thing does not happen, because a seventy – eighty-years-old person retains a major part of memories of dangers that have passed on him. He can recall the memory and recognize that they are the same dangers that passed on him. Such a thing is not compatible with materiality of memory! This can lead us to conclude that memory (imagination) is an abstract and non-material thing and in fact it is the intellect of man that in the stage of imagination perceives partial forms and meanings and retains them in the archives of his memory. This can also lead us to discover the abstractness and non-materiality of the self of man. Rising of the forms and meanings are matters, which are perceptible by the intellect of man also are originative rising and not transmigrative or reactionary.

So far we have learnt three reasonings from the reasoning of the abstractness of the soul:

1. Innate knowledge of the self with regard to itself.
2. Knowledge of the self with the generalities.
3. Knowledge of the self through forms and partial meanings stored in the memory.

More arguments are offered on the abstractness of the soul in books of philosophy, but we shall be content only with these.[11]

---

[11] Refer to Asfar, Vol. 2

Soul in the Quran

In order to identify the viewpoint of Islam with regard to the reality of the self of man we can utilize three types of verses:

First type: Verses related to death. In some verses, the Almighty Allah has compared death to 'Tawafi' (taking up). For example:

> "And He it is Who takes your souls at night (in sleep), and He knows what you acquire in the day, then He raises you up therein that an appointed term may be fulfilled; then to Him is your return, then He will inform you of what you were doing. And He is the Supreme, above His servants, and He sends keepers over you; until when death comes to one of you, Our messengers cause him to die, and they are not remiss." (6:60-61)

"And they say: What! when we have become lost in the earth,

shall we then certainly be in a new creation? Nay! they are disbelievers in the meeting of their Lord. Say: The angel of death who is given charge of you shall cause you to die, then to your Lord you shall be brought back." (32:10-11)

"Allah takes the souls at the time of their death, and those that die not during their sleep; then He withholds those on whom He has passed the decree of death and sends the others back till an appointed term; most surely there are signs in this for a people who reflect."(39:42)

In the above verses and other similar ones, death is describes as the taking up of the souls, which is accomplished by the Almighty Allah and the angel of death (Malakul Maut). Thus Raghib Isfahani has stated that 'Tawaffi' implies taking up of the reality of a thing completely. In the above mentioned verses, death of man is explained in such a way that when the death of a person approaches his worldly reality is completely taken up through the Almighty Allah and the angel of death and nothing from it is wasted. That which is taken up leaving nothing behind is nothing but the soul of man. If man had been only a body without a soul, nothing would have remained that it should be taken up by the Almighty Allah and the angels, as the body of every man after death will decay and deteriorate. Thus the addressee in these verses is the same abstract soul of man.

Numerous traditions also prove the same point. For example:

Hanan bin Sudair has narrated from his father that he said:

I was with Imam Ja'far Sadiq ('a) when mention was made of a believer and his rights. Thus His Eminence said to me: "O Abul Fadhl, should I not inform you about the position of a believer in the view of Allah?"

I said: "May I be your ransom, please do tell me."

He said:

"When the Almighty Allah captures the soul of a believer, the two angels appointed on him ascend to the heavens and plead before the Almighty Allah: 'O Lord, Your servant was the best of servants and he obeyed You most readily and refrained from Your disobedience. Then You have taken him to Yourself. Now what do You command us with regard to him?' The Almighty Allah tells them: **'Go back to the earth and remain besides his grave worshipping Me and recite supplications and write their rewards in the scroll of deed of My servant till I raise him up again.'**"[12]

Second type: Verses which state that after death, man will return to the Almighty Allah. There are a large number of verses of this type:

"He gives life and causes death, and to Him you shall be brought back." (10:56)

"Every soul must taste of death, then to Us you shall be brought back." (29:57)

"...To Allah is your return, of all (of you), so He will inform you of what you did." (5:105)

Such verses show that all human beings will return to the Almighty Allah. It is known that returning can be imagined only when the same person who lived in world, remains and then returns to Allah. If man had been only this material body, which decays after death and if

---

[12] Biharul Anwar, Vol. 6, Pg. 152

nothing known as soul had existed, return to Allah would have been meaningless as the body of man is not capable of returning.

Third type: Verses revealed about the creation of Adam and the blowing of the sprit of God into him. For example:

> *"When your Lord said to the angels; Surely I am going to create a mortal from dust: So when I have made him complete and breathed into him of My spirit, then fall down making obeisance to him." (38:71-72)*

> *"(It is He) Who made good everything that He has created, and He began the creation of man from dust. Then He made his progeny of an extract of water held in light estimation. Then He made him complete and breathed into him of His spirit, and made for you the ears and the eyes and the hearts; little is it that you give thanks." (32:7-9)*

In the above mentioned verses, the blowing of the spirit of God into the body of man is regarded as his excellence, because the angels were asked to prostrate before man and pay obeisance to him. The word of soul is used in many occasions in the Holy Quran and the above verse is one of them. People asked the Messenger of Allah (s) about the reality of the soul and the following verse was revealed in reply:

> *"And they ask you about the soul. Say: The soul is one of the commands of my Lord, and you are not given aught of knowledge but a little." (17:85)*

In another verse is explained the 'command of Allah' as follows:

> *"His command, when He intends anything, is only to say to it: Be, so it is. Therefore glory be to Him in Whose hand is the kingdom of all things, and to Him you shall be brought back." (36:82-83)*

This verse mentions the act of creation by the Almighty Allah that is not gradual and timely, but that it is abstract and that He only says: Be and it comes into existence immediately and it simpler words it can be said that the creation of every phenomenon is in fact its existence.

All the phenomena in the world are created by the Almighty Allah. So much so, that we have two types of phenomena and two kinds of creations: material and abstract. The Almighty Allah brings into existence the material phenomena through the medium of cause and effects; this type of creation is called as 'Creation' (Khalq) in the Holy Quran and they are produced in time and in gradual stages. But there are no stages in the creation of abstract phenomena and it is not bound by time.

In such instances, terms like 'originating' and 'initiating' is used. Such phenomena are considered to be from the world of command; that is they have come into being merely by the Almighty Allah saying: Be! But to be more accurate, one should say: In creation of material things also there is no graduality from the Almighty Allah and it is only through the command of 'Be'; and if there are stages, they are only in the causes and in the acquisition of capabilities and not in the creation and action of the Almighty Allah as proved by the statement of:

> *"..In Whose hand is the kingdom of all things." (23:88)*

Kingdoms and unseen parts of all things are under the discretion of the Lord of the worlds and it is created and organized through His innate intention.

One of the implications of abstract things is the soul and spirit of man. But this abstract as opposed to other abstract things has two aspects: physical and material, which is related to his body; that is why the word of 'creation' is used in its creating. And second is the aspect of abstraction and spirituality, which is mentioned in the phrase of 'I blew my soul in him' and the phrase of 'then We caused it to grow into another creation' is used in this regard. Pay attention to the following verse:

> *"And certainly We created man of an extract of clay. Then We made him a small seed in a firm resting-place. Then We made the seed a clot, then We made the clot a lump of flesh, then We made (in) the lump of flesh bones, then We clothed the bones with flesh, then We caused it to grow into another creation, so blessed be Allah, the best of the creators."* (23:11-14)

In the first part of this verse are mentioned the initial stages and movements of gaining capability and physical perfections in the creation of man and that is why the word of 'creation' is used. But when the soul of man is mentioned, the phrase of "then We caused it to grow into another creation" is used in order to declare its superiority over other phenomena. It is about this special creation that it is said:

> *"Blessed be Allah, the best of the creators."*

From what is stated above, it can be concluded that the soul of man in the view of Islam is an existing thing, which is abstract and superior to material matter that does not decay after death. On the contrary it is transferred from this world to the perpetual world of the hereafter so that it may be rewarded or punished according to its good or bad deeds.

Death and its hardships

We don't have proper knowledge of the reality of death, because the reality of life is also unknown to us. Our understanding with regard to these two important matters is only to the limit of their traces not more. A phenomenon, which has a particular condition and which carries the qualities of nutrition, growth and reproduction is considered by us to be a living being. In some beings, in addition to this, we consider perception and voluntary movement as signs of life. In man, in addition to these, we consider acquisition of intelligence, contemplation and speech as additional signs of life; but all of these are signs of life and not its reality. Death is also like this and any living phenomena, which loses the signs of its life is said to be dead. But these are signs of death and not its reality. The reality of death is unknown. According to the Holy Quran, life and death are two created things created by the Almighty Allah.

The Holy Quran says:

"(It is He) Who created death and life that He may try you-

which of you is best in deeds; and He is the Mighty, the Forgiving." (67:2)

It is known that only an existing matter can be created and not an inexistent matter. What is remarkable in this verse is that death is mentioned before life. That which can be stated about death and life is that the soul of man is having two stages of existence. The soul of man in the stage of life is of the type which is in need of a material body to continue its life and to reach to its perfection and it is having a particular life. But after death it is able to live on its own without a material body. In this stage it would have another life, which is very much opposed to the past life and most important of all, it is an everlasting life.

In both conditions it is one person and not more. The Messenger of Allah (s) has stated:

"Death is the first stage in the stages of the hereafter and the last stage from the stages of the world."[13]

Imam Khomeini says:

Death is the transfer of man from the apparent proprietary formation to the unseen celestial formation; along with the fact that death is second celestial life, after the first proprietary life and in any case is an existing matter. On the contrary it is the most perfect proprietary existence, because the worldly proprietary life contaminated with the substance of death, and their life is a passing accident as opposed to the natural celestial life, which in such circumstances is present in independent souls and it is the abode of life and a necessary component of life.[14]

He also says:

Seed (sperm) is in motion within its essence and continues to undergo

---

[13] Biharul Anwar, Vol. 6, Pg. 133

[14] Maad az Deedgah Imam Khomeini, Pg. 137

transformations, till finally its form is changed into the soul. The soul also satiated with essence is in constant motion till it reaches different stages and ranks of abstraction, although its nature is present in the stages of its existence; but as result of its continuous substantial motion its abstraction goes on increasing and its natural aspect goes on decreasing and finally it pulls out itself from nature. This presence, in which stage it takes out itself from nature is in fact the same previous natural form which arose due to its substantial motion and in every step freed itself from one stage of its nature. When it finally frees its whole existence from the shackles of nature, it becomes independent and its independence is that it has freed itself from nature for the last time, and becoming independent is same as coming out of the nature. Death of man follows the independence of the soul and not that it is by chance and then man comes out of the nature; the independence which has actualized is in the meaning of emerging and emerging from the nature is in the same sense.[15]

Throes of Death

It is learnt from verses of Quran and traditions that death is accompanied with great pain, which is mentioned in Quran as Sakara and Ghamara (stupor/agony of death).

The Holy Quran says:

"And the stupor of death will come in truth; that is what you were trying to escape." (Surah Qaf 50:19)

And also says:

"..and if you had seen when the unjust shall be in the agonies

---

[15] Maad az Deedgah Imam Khomeini, Pg. 138

> *of death and the angels shall spread forth their hands: Give up your souls; today shall you be recompensed with an ignominious chastisement..." (6:93)*

Stupor and agony are used in the meaning of a senseless state, which is due to the severity of those circumstances. In these verses they are interpreted to be the hardships of death. The hardships of death are not physical pains and discomfort; on the contrary it is spiritual and internal and it is much more severe than physical tortures. Physical pains are felt through senses and they reach the soul from this channel, but spiritual and internal chastisements scorch the being.

Hardships of death can be from various aspects:

1. Attachment to what he has gathered in his life: Like the house, property, wealth, children and other worldly things. Man struggled all his life to obtain them and committed lawful and unlawful acts in their pursuit with the hope that they would give him some advantage at the end of his life. Their love had taken a deep root in his being that it is very difficult for him to ignore them now. At the time of death, he sees that he would be compelled to leave every worldly thing to which he was attached and move to the everlasting world of the hereafter empty-handed.

2. Seeing his past deeds: Throughout his life man continues to commit numerous small and big sins and after sometime forgets most of them in such a way that as if he had never committed them. He does not even recall them in order to repent for them. While the fact is that all his words, acts and morals are recorded in the scroll of his deeds and these same deeds have earned for him Hell and the chastisement of Hell. At the time of death, the curtain will be removed from his eyes and he will see each act committed by him during his lifespan and the recompense of the same. And how severe it would be for one to see all one has committed in his lifespan in an instant?

The Holy Quran says:

> "On the day that every soul shall find present what it has done of good and what it has done of evil, it shall wish that between it and that (evil) there were a long duration of time; and Allah makes you to be cautious of (retribution from) Himself; and Allah is Compassionate to the servants." (3:30)

3. Seeing his bad position in the everlasting world of the hereafter: A sinner or one who is basically not having faith in Allah, the hereafter and sayings of prophets; in such a way that his expression of faith was only formal and not rooted in his being and that is why he justified his offensive acts and always contented himself with vain and useless hopes and some of his minor acts and was uncaring about the imminent consequences of the hereafter. But as mentioned in traditions, at the time of death, the curtain will be removed from the conscience of man during the throes of death and in one instant he would see with his own eyes, his position in the hereafter as well as the consequences of all his deeds, views and behavior and also observe all his hopes being dashed and he would pass away in that condition. And how difficult dying is in this condition!

4. Cutting off perpetual relations: Another reason for the hardship of a dying person and his opposition to physical pain is that in physical pains, one or more organs feel the pain and transfer the stages of their restlessness to the soul, but at the time of death, the human man desires to cut off forever its connection with all the organs and limbs. And this is but a very difficult task.

That which was stated above was about infidels, oppressors and sinners, but as mentioned in traditions, death for the righteous believers is not only not hard, on the contrary, it is very pleasant and nice. The

Holy Quran says:

> *"O soul that are at rest! Return to your Lord, well-pleased (with him), well-pleasing (Him), So enter among My servants, And enter into My garden." (89:27-30)*

It was said to Imam Ja'far Sadiq ('a): "Please explain death to us."

He replied:

"For the believer, it is like a nice fragrance, which comforts him and cures all his pains. But death for a disbeliever would be like the sting of a snake or scorpion; on the contrary it would be much more severe."[16]

Imam Hasan ('a) was asked: "What is death?"

He replied:

"It is greatest happiness that would be bestowed to the believers when they would be transferred from the world full of hardships to the bounties of the everlasting world. And it is the great destruction that would befall the disbelievers, when they would be transferred from their worldly paradise to the everlasting fire (of Hell)."[17]

The Messenger of Allah (s) said:

"People are of two kinds, one is those from whom others will get relief and the other kind are those who would get the relief themselves. Those who get the relief themselves are believers. When death approaches them they would get relief from hardships and pains of this world. And those from whom others would get relief are the disbelievers. When they die, the trees, animals and a large number of people would get relief from them."[18]

---

[16] Biharul Anwar, Vol. 6, Pg. 152

[17] Biharul Anwar, Vol. 6, Pg. 154

[18] Biharul Anwar, Vol. 6, Pg. 151

Imam Sajjad ('a) was asked: "What is death?"

He replied:

"For the believer it is like the taking off of a dirty garment and an iron collar and chain; changing into the nicest garments, the most fragrant perfumes and riding the best mount and the best of the abodes. For the disbeliever, it is like taking off the garment of pride and transfer from the best abodes into the filthiest and the roughest garments and into the most terrifying houses and to the most severe chastisements."[19]

Imam Muhammad Baqir ('a) said:

"At the time of death, the angel of death says: 'What you hope for will be given to you and that from which you fear, you will be given security.' At that moment, a door to Paradise will be opened before him and he will see his position. He would be told, 'Look at your abode in Paradise and look at the Prophet, Ali, Hasan and Husain ('a); they are your neighbors.' This is statement of the Almighty Allah in the Holy Quran:

> *"Those who believe and guarded (against evil): they shall have good news in this world's life and in the hereafter."* **(10:63-64)**[20]

From the above mentioned traditions and tens of others like them, it becomes clear that righteous believers having faith in Allah, the Prophet and the Judgment Day, and who perform their religious duties, not only will they be safe from the agonies of death, on the contrary, at the time of death, they would see their position in Paradise and their life in the neighborhood of the Prophet and the Holy Imams ('a). And with most satisfaction and absolute free will and with the recommendation

---

[19] Biharul Anwar, Vol. 6, Pg. 155

[20] Biharul Anwar, Vol. 6, Pg. 177

of the Prophet and the affections of the angel of death, they surrender their lives and hasten to the everlasting world to meet their Lord. They are released from a world replete with sorrow and grief, hardships and problems, injustice and inequity, pain and diseases and transferred to a world full of effulgence and happiness and life in neighborhood of the chosen servants of the Almighty Allah, where they might enjoy the choicest divine bounties. How sweet and pleasant is dying in this way! Believers are not attached to this world that they should fear being separated from it. They have not committed sins that they should be terrified of its consequences in the hereafter; even if they have committed some sinful acts in ignorance, they have repented for it and have got it erased from the scroll of their deeds. They have improved their hereafter with meritorious deeds and good morals and have been honored in the view of the Prophet and the Holy Imams ('a); therefore why should they fear death? Hence the friends of God do not seek to evade death; on the contrary they hasten to it eagerly.

Although it is not that all believers would be safe from agonies of death, on the contrary, the sinners among them who died without repenting – proportionate to their attachment to the world and depending on the magnitude of their sins – they would have to taste the agonies of death, but not as much as infidels and oppressors. In the same way, all disbelievers and oppressors also would not be same from the aspect of suffering the agonies of death.

It is said that the bitterness of dying is other than the pain and discomfort suffered by those who are ill at the time of their death. It is not that if the righteous believer has been on the sick bed for a long time, this suffering can be counted as the agonies of death; on the contrary the dying of this person would be in the same meaning as stated before; with his approval and by his free will. On the other hand, it is not that if a disbeliever or an oppressor dies in an instant, we should say that he did not have to taste the agonies of death.

In the Grave

Questioning in the Grave

Muslims believe that after the dead is buried in the grave, divinely appointed interrogating angels arrive and ask the deceased about his faith and beliefs; if he had been a righteous believer, a door to Paradise is opened before him and he would enjoy the bounties of Paradise till Judgment Day; and if he had been a disbeliever or an oppressor, a door to Hell will opened before him and he will continue to suffer the chastisement of Hell till Judgment Day. In fact there is no doubt in this, because a large number of traditions are recorded about it and we present some of them by way of examples.

Imam Ja'far Sadiq ('a) said: "One who denies three things is not amongst our Shia (i.e. followers and devotees): Ascension of the Prophet, questioning of the grave, and intercession."[21]

Imam Musa Kazim ('a) has narrated from his father, Imam Ja'far Sadiq ('a), that he said:

---

[21] Biharul Anwar, Vol. 6, Pg. 223

"When a believer dies, seventy thousand angels participate in his funeral; when he enters the grave, Munkir and Nakeer come to him and pose questions to him; they ask him: 'Who is your god? What is your religion? And who is your prophet?' The believer replies: 'My Lord is Allah, my prophet is Muḥammad, and my religion is Islam.' At that moment the grave is expanded as far as the eye can see and the foods of Paradise will be brought there for him and the breeze of Paradise will welcome him. It is this, which is mentioned in the Holy Quran:

"If he is one of those drawn nigh (to Allah), then happiness and bounty and a garden of bliss (shall be his)." (56:88-89)
"...That is in the grave and Paradise of bliss, that is in the hereafter."

Then the Imam said:

"When a disbeliever dies, seventy thousand angels of Hell accompany him to the grave. In this condition the dead person will plead to them in a voice, which would be audible to all except humans and jinns: 'If only I had been able to return to the world and had become of the faithful.' And he says: 'Send me back to the world, perhaps I may do good in that, which I have left.' Angels of Hell would say: 'By no means! It is a (mere) word that you speak,' and one of the angels would say: 'If you are sent back to the world, you will again do the same.' When his dead body is interred and people go away from there, Nakeer and Munkar come to him in the most terrible form and they raise him up for questioning. They ask him: 'Who is your god? What is your religion? And who is your prophet?' Since the disbeliever had no sincere faith in them, he would stammer and fail to reply. Thus those two angels would lash him in a punishment that everything will be terrified of it.

They would ask him: 'Who is your god? What is your religion? And who is your prophet?' He would reply: 'I don't know.' So they would tell him: 'Neither you know, nor you were guided to the right path.' Thus a door would be opened to Hell before him and the scalding fluids of Hell would come down to him. It is about this that is mentioned in the Holy Quran:

> **"And if he is one of the rejecters, the erring ones. He shall have an entertainment of boiling water..." (56:92-93)**
> *That is, in the grave he would be greeted by boiling water,* **"And burning in hell." (56:94)**
> *That is, in the hereafter, he would be consigned to Hell."*[22]

Imam Ali ('a) said:

"When the corpse is interred, two angels, named Munkir and Nakeer arrive. Their first questions to the dead are about God, prophet and caliphs. If it replies correctly, it is given salvation and if it is unable to reply correctly, they punish it."[23]

Tens of other traditions also mention the same points, but quoting all of them here would prolong the discussion.

Squeeze of the Grave

Squeeze of the Grave is a painful event, which is mentioned in some traditions and the Infallibles ('a) have also informed about it. For example:

Amirul Momineen ('a) wrote to Muhammad bin Abu Bakr:

"O people, events occurring after death are more severe than death itself. Beware of the squeeze of the grave and the darkness and

---

[22] Biharul Anwar, Vol. 6, Pg. 222

[23] Biharul Anwar, Vol. 6, Pg. 233

loneliness in it. The grave calls out everyday: I am the house of strangeness, a house of dust, abode of loneliness and the house of stinging creatures. Grave is either a garden from the gardens of Paradise or a pit from the pits of Hell. When a believer is buried, the grave says: Welcome, previously I was desirous that you would walk to me, now that you are entrusted to me, you will see how I behave with you. At that moment the grave will be expanded as far as the eye can see. But when a disbeliever is buried, the earth says: You are not welcome. Before this I detested your coming to me. Now that you are in my custody, you will see how I deal with you. At that moment he would be squeezed in such a way that his bones will merge into each other. A life of hardships that the Almighty Allah has promised to the disbelievers in the grave includes ninety-nine large serpents who will chew his flesh and crush his bones. This will continue till Judgment Day. If one of those large serpents were to blow on the earth, nothing would ever grow on it again. O people, protect your weak selves and bodies that have lived in a tender way. Protect your bodies from the hardships, which they are unable to bear. Do that which the Almighty Allah likes and keep away from acts, which He has prohibited."[24]

The Holy Prophet (s) remarked about cause of the squeeze of grave that Saad had to suffer: "He was harsh and bad-tempered with his wife."[25]

The Messenger of Allah (s) said: "Squeeze of grave is due to wasting of the bounties."[26]

It is because of such traditions that most scholars have concluded that faith in questioning of grave is a fundamental principle of Islamic faith. Mulla Mohsin Faiz Kashani writes:

---

[24] Biharul Anwar, Vol. 6, Pg. 218
[25] Biharul Anwar, Vol. 6, Pg. 217
[26] Biharul Anwar, Vol. 6, Pg. 221

Questioning, and punishment and reward of the grave is one of the necessary fundamentals of Islamic faith since there are a large number of traditions in this regard in Shia and Sunni sources, which remove every kind of doubt about it.[27]

Shaykh Tusi writes in Tajreedul Itiqad:

Chastisement of the grave is definite and imminent and also an inordinate number of traditions have come down about it from Ahle Bayt ('a).[28]

The chastisement of Purgatory (Barzakh) and its rewards are matters on which Muslims have consensus.[29]

Therefore questioning and chastisement of the grave should not be doubted about; however its actual process requires discussion and research.

Whether man would hear the questions posed by the angels through these same worldly ears and would he reply through this same tongue or it is through some other types?

How is it possible for a body, which has lost the functioning of the heart, brain, organs, ears, eyes, tongue and other limbs and which has cooled down to hear the questions of the angels with the ears and how is it possible to answer them with the tongue?

Moreover, angels who are from the non-material spiritual world would they ask with the same worldly tongue so that the dead person may hear them with the same worldly ears and reply with the same tongue? Speaking of the angels is of another kind, which cannot be heard by worldly ears. Jibraeel used speak to the Prophet, but those around him were unable to hear it.

The Holy Prophet (s) used to hear Jibraeel through his inward ears

---

[27] Mulla Mohsin Kashani, Ilmul Yaqeen, Vol. 2, Pg. 873

[28] Allamah Hilli, Kashful Murad Fee Sharhe Tajreedul Itiqaad, Pg. 424

[29] Haqqul Yaqeen, Vol. 2, Pg. 68

and spoke to him with his inward tongue. Questioning of the angels must also be of this type. Angels speak to the abstract soul of man. He also hears the questions of the angels through his spiritual ears and replies with his inward tongue. That is why, if voice control is overlooked in the grave, he will not have to control it.

Rewards and punishments of grave should also be of such kind. This dusty grave, which is not expanded and a door is not opened from Paradise in his direction, so that bounties of Paradise may arrive there. Since the useless body of the dead also does not need nutrition. Therefore the grave should be related to the soul and its abode. Chastisements of the grave should also be of the same type. In this pit, where the corpse was buried, there is neither scorpion nor huge vipers or stinging creatures; even if they were present and were also to sting the dead body, what can a lifeless body feel? Therefore harmful creatures of the grave should be such that they can hurt the soul of the dead and only this much is sufficient in the chastisement of the grave. Spiritual and sensual punishment is definitely more severe than physical chastisements.

In physical chastisements also, that which suffers is actually the soul. In this earthly grave, no squeeze and fire of Hell is experienced, therefore the grave mentioned in the traditions must be some other place.

That grave is the abode of the soul and not the body; therefore it can be said that the first grave implies the abode of the soul after death; that is the beginning of entry into the Purgatory (Barzakh). But since this transfer is contemporary with the entry of the body into the earthly grave, it is interpreted as grave. Therefore one who drowns or one whose body is cut up into pieces, or one who is burnt or becomes dust, he also has to face questioning of the grave and would feel the pleasures of Paradise and the punishments of Hell.

In some traditions also grave is interpreted in this way. For example:

The Messenger of Allah (s) said:

"Grave is the first stage of the hereafter. If man is able to get salvation in that stage, the later stages would be easier for him, but if he is unable to get salvation in that stage, he would be more unlikely to get salvation after that."[30]

Imam Sajjad ('a) said after reciting the verse of:

"...And before them is a barrier until the day they are raised." (23:100)

"Barzakh is the grave. Indeed for them there is a hard life there. By Allah, the grave is either a garden from the gardens of Paradise or a pit from the pits of Hell."[31]

Allamah Majlisi writes:

"Grave in most traditions implies the world of Barzakh, where the soul of man is transferred."[32]

Allamah Tabatabai has written in the marginal notes of Biharul Anwar as follows:

Perhaps it implies that after death, man would not be destroyed completely. On the contrary, it implies another life other than the life he has lost. As the Messenger of Allah (s) has said: 'And indeed they would be transferred from one abode to another'. But the traditional report which apparently states that in the grave, the soul would re-enter the body of the dead upto his knees, is figurative. For questioning in the grave since the statements in these same traditions are from the sayings of the angels that they would tell the believer: 'Go to sleep like a bride,' is figurative for the stay of the believer in the grave waiting for

---

[30] Biharul Anwar, Vol. 6, Pg. 242

[31] Biharul Anwar, Vol. 6, Pg. 214

[32] Biharul Anwar, Vol. 6, Pg. 271

Qiyamat.[33]

Imam Khomeini writes with regard to this:

"But this does not mean that all the graves would be abodes of questioning and comfort for the believer. The grave, which has questions and answers or pain and sorrow or happiness and joy; does not have the natural form; on the contrary it has the form of Barzakh and the facsimile world. Attachment and attention to the abode of nature exists as long as the self is in the Barzakh and the world of grave. Expansion and squeeze in this world is under the control of the expansion and squeeze of the chest and self of man. But a grave, which is one and a half metre in length and half a metre in width is not the same grave about which it is said that it is: between the east and the west or for example no matter how much we search in these graves, we would never find pythons in them.[34]

---

[33] Biharul Anwar, Vol. 6, Pg. 280

[34] Maad az Deedgah Imam Khomeini, Pg. 171

Purgatory (Barzakh)

It is learnt from a large number of verses of Quran and traditions that death is not the end of the life of man, on the contrary, after death he is transferred to another world called Barzakh and he continues his life there. The world of Barzakh is between the perceptive world of this life and the world of the hereafter and complete gathering. The world of Barzakh begins from the grave and it continues till the complete gathering and the establishment of Judgment Day. But it is not transmigration in which the soul of man enters the body of another man or animal. And after his death, he enters another body…and in this way he continues his life so that he may be cleaned of filths and become fully eligible for the gathering of Judgment Day. Belief in transmigration of souls is absurd and incompatible with principles of Islam.

In the beginning we would present some verses of Quran with regard to Barzakh as examples:

The Holy Quran says:

"Until when death overtakes one of them, he says: Send me back, my Lord, send me back; haply I may do good in that which I have left. By no means! it is a (mere) word that he speaks; and before them is a barrier until the day they are raised." (23:99-100)

"And reckon not those who are killed in Allah's way as dead; nay, they are alive (and) are provided sustenance from their Lord; Rejoicing in what Allah has given them out of His grace and they rejoice for the sake of those who, (being left) behind them, have not yet joined them, that they shall have no fear, nor shall they grieve." (3:169-170)

In these verses, it is clearly mentioned that martyrs are alive after death and it cannot be interpreted as immortality of their name and cause, although life after death is different from the life of the world. If we accept life after death for the martyrs, we would have to accept life for all the other people as well. The difference of martyrs to other people is that the martyrs are sustained by their Lord in that elevated stage. They receive sustenance from the Almighty Allah.

Therefore, it must be said: All the people are also alive after death and they are transferred to a world called Barzakh and they continue their life there. Numerous traditions also imply this point. For example:

Abu Walad says: I asked Imam Ja'far Sadiq ('a): "May I be your ransom, it is narrated that after death the souls of the believers will be placed in the gizzard of green colored birds. And they will circulate around the throne of Almighty."

He replied:

"No, it is not so. The believer is more exalted that his soul should be placed in the gizzard of fowls. On the contrary, the souls of believers will be in bodies like the bodies of this world."³⁵

Yunus says: I was with Imam Ja'far Sadiq ('a) when he asked: "What do people say about the souls of believers?"

I said: "They say that they would be placed in crops of green birds, in the lanterns hanging below the Arsh."

He said:

"Glory be to Allah! A believer is more respectable than that his soul should be placed in crop of birds. O Yunus, when the death of a believer approaches, the Holy Prophet (s), Ali, Fatima, Hasan and Husain ('a) and the proximate angels of the Almighty Allah appear to him and when the Almighty Allah captures his soul, He places it in a body, which is like the worldly body. Thus he eats and drinks. When the fresh soul enters it, they recognize him in the same form as he was having in the world."³⁶

Abu Basir has narrated from Imam Ja'far Sadiq ('a) that he said:

"Souls of believers live in form of bodies between the trees of Paradise. They introduce and speak to each other. When a new soul enters, they remark to each other: Leave him/her; he just escaped a great terror. After that they ask him: How is so-and-so person? If he replies: He is alive. They hope for his salvation and if he says that he is dead, they say: He has gone into perdition."³⁷

Such traditions and some traditions we mentioned in the discussion of grave show that that the souls of man after death are transferred to a world called Barzakh. And in that world they possess a physical body, which is exactly like the body of this world, in such a way that those who know him would recognize him and speak to him.

Therefore the soul of man in Barzakh has a body, but it is not the

---

³⁵ Biharul Anwar, Vol. 6, Pg. 267

³⁶ Biharul Anwar, Vol. 6, Pg. 269

³⁷ Biharul Anwar, Vol. 6, Pg. 269

body of the world, since if it had been worldly, it would not have been of the Barzakh and the hereafter.

Barzakhi Body

Now the question arises that where is the body of Barzakh located and how it comes into being till the soul of the dead after separating from the worldly body, is placed in it? Do previously created bodies exist in the world of Barzakh without any owners so that the soul may choose one for itself? Or that the soul has a Barzakhi body in the world, and after death it is taken along with it?

The first possibility is untenable, because on the basis of this supposition, the Barzakhi body is not a worldly body, through which man performs good deeds and commits evil deeds, in order to become eligible for good rewards or bad consequences. Additionally, what need does the soul of man have –along with perfect abstractness and after leaving the worldly body– that it should be placed in a pre-fabricated Barzakhi body, which is also not his worldly body?

Thus on the basis of this and traditions mentioned above, it can be said that the soul of man in this world itself has a Barzakhi body, which he takes away with itself to the world of Barzakh. The greatest philosophers of Islam, like Mulla Sadra, have this belief and they have defended it. But imagining and testifying it is very difficult. In my view, it is best to leave the decision of this important matter to Mulla Sadra, who is among the most senior scholars on this topic and directly refer to his statement. This great philosopher has investigated all the dimensions of this problem at various places in his Asfar and has expressed his view about it. To mention all of them in this brief writing is impossible. Here we shall mention two of his statements:

The first occurrence or priority of the self:

Some say: Souls of human beings were created before their bodies and they are infinitely pre-existent and non-material. Whenever a matter from the world becomes capable to accept the soul, a soul is placed in it and benefits from it in gaining perfections, like a sailor who guides the ship and conveys it to its destination. And when he does not need it or the ship becomes useless and old, he abandons it. But researchers from Islamic philosophers, for example Sadruddin Shirazi considers this view absurd. He refutes this theory as follows:

If the soul of man had been pre-existing infinitely, it should have been perfect and defect-less in the stage of being and free from materiality and if it was perfect, it would not have been in need of association with the body, and use of vegetative and animal instruments and capacities. Moreover, if the abstract was perfect and infinitely pre-existing, the human form would have been limited to one person, since multiplicity is a sign of matter.[38]

He considers the soul of man to be a thing created by the body; that when the matter of the body of man by substantial motion (Harkat Jauhari) and bodily changes reaches to a limit where it is able to accept the human soul; its last form of physical matter changes into the human soul. In this regard he writes:

From the aspect of being created and control of body, the human soul is physical and from the aspect of survival and intellect, it is spiritual.[39]

In the same way, he writes about the connection of the soul to the body:

The connection of the soul to the body is accidental from the aspect of being and identification of the occurrence, but it is not so from the aspect of survival. The soul of man in the beginning of creation was having the quality of material natures as it was in need of vague matter. The soul, in the beginning of creation, is also in need of vague bodily matter, since the body of man throughout his life, is under constant

---

[38] Asfar, Vol. 8, Pg. 331, Part 1 of Fourth Journey

[39] Asfar, Vol. 8, Pg. 347, Part 1 of Fourth Journey

change and variable quantum. Therefore the person of man, although it is a single individual from the aspect of spirituality and not more; but from the aspect of physicality in the sense of substance and not in the sense of kind or sort – is a not a single person.[40]

On another occasion, he writes:

The soul of man is having ranks and personal and existential signs, some of which are from the world of command and destiny. Thus the Holy Quran says:

"Say: The soul is one of the commands of my Lord..." (17:85)

Some of it is from the world of creation and forms; hence it is mentioned in Quran:

"From it We created you and into it We shall send you back and from it will We raise you a second time." (20:55)

Thus incidentality and invention is among the signs of some ranks of the soul. Therefore we say: Since the soul of man itself has progressed from the first creation to another creation on the path of development as the Quran has mentioned:

"And certainly We created you, then We fashioned you, then We said to the angels: Make obeisance to Adam." (7:11)

Thus when he progressed from the world of creation and arose to

---

[40] Asfar, Vol. 8, Pg. 326, Part 1 of Fourth Journey

the world of command its being became the being of a separate intellectuality which had no need of the body and its actions and capacities. Therefore with regard to the soul, it must be said: From the aspect of incidentally, it is physical but from the aspect of survival it is spiritual.[41]

The following important points can be concluded from these statements:

1. The human soul is not created as an infinitely pre-existing and an abstract thing; on the contrary it is a newly created phenomenon from the physical phenomenon. In the sense that when the matter of the body of man, through substantial motion reached to a stage of perfection where it became capable to accept the human soul, the last physical form changed into the abstract human soul. However, the soul at this time is still having potentiality related to the perception of sciences. It can become further perfect along with the body and could actively change the capacity to perceive sciences and generalities.

Thus man consists of a physical body and an abstract celestial soul and the two are integrated and possess a single existence and identity.

2. The human soul from the aspect of incidentality and development of the being is having ranks of existence. Its lowest stage is that which has a connection with a material and physical body and is considered to be from the world of creation, as mentioned in Quran; and its highest stage is abstract and celestial and it is considered to be from the world of command.

3. It is correct that human soul is in need of a physical body in its incidentality, continuation of its existence and its development, is in need of a physical body, but the body with regard to its need is not permanent and unchangeable, on the contrary, it is a fluid body, which is situated between two limits: in the beginning of which is childhood

---

[41] Asfar, Vol. 8, Pg. 393, Part 1 of Fourth Journey

and in the end is the end of worldly life. Even though the fluids of the human body due to the effect of nutrition are under constant and continuous change, but this matter does not damage the individuality of the soul and the physical body.

Barzakhi Body in different opinions

Mulla Sadra is of the view that the Barzakhi body is an advanced stage of this same worldly body, which after death is transferred to the world of Barzakh along with the soul of man. With regard to this, he writes:

We should know that man is a compound of the soul and body, and these two, in spite of differences from the aspect of status and position are present in a single existence. In such a way that it can be said that they are a single, which has two stages and two-sided existence. One of its stages is having change, it becomes old and it perishes, but this stage is a secondary dimension of man and not his primary aspect. Another stage of the body, which is also his reality; is permanent and everlasting. As much the human soul becomes more perfect in its being the body which is connected to it also becomes finer and lighter and its contact with the soul becomes stronger and union of the two becomes more intense; in such a way that when it rises to the stage of the intellectual existence, the soul and the body become a single reality in every sense. Some philosophers are of the view that worldly change and existence of the soul in spite of its supernatural existence is that the worldly body is taken up by it. In the same way, as man comes out of his garments and becomes naked. But this belief is not correct. Their misunderstanding is due to the fact that they think that the natural body of man, which is directly under the control and will of the soul, is the same material body which is separated and released from it. But this belief is incorrect. This material body is not directly under the control of the soul, on the contrary its ranks as refuse and staying under the filths and dirts of human body or by the rank of sheep wool and the horn and hooves of cow, sheep and camels that are not part of their actual body and according to another view, the created body of man is also same. The material body can be considered to be in the rank of a house that a man constructs in order to protect himself from summer and winter and to fulfill his other needs. He lives in it, but it is not a part of his body.

The actual human body is same that within it runs the effulgence of perception and innate life, and not a body with supposed feeling and life. The relation of the actual body to the soul is like the relation of light to the sun, which was always with it and had never been separated from it. If life of this cut-off body had been a part of its being, it would not have decomposed and abandoned after death.

Summarily, the soul in the stages of abstraction is an external phenomenon, which in the beginning can be perceived through apparent senses. After that it is stored in memory and in the end it assumes the form of a rational thing. According to philosophers:

Every perception having a kind of abstraction with itself and its stages of perceptions are according to the stages of abstraction; is also in the same meaning; and that it is said: Abstraction of a perceptive thing is not in this meaning; that in abstraction of some qualities of the perceptive thing are cut off and some of them remain. On the contrary, abstraction means: transformation of insignificant and defective into a loftier and nobler existence. In the same way, the being of man and his transfer from the world to the hereafter is nothing other than that his worldly constitution is changed into the life of the hereafter. In the same way, the perfection of the human soul and the actualization of his intellect is not that some of his capacities like feelings etc, should be taken from him and his intellect remains intact, on the contrary as much he is perfected and his being scales higher stages, his capacities also become perfect and exalted. Since as much the being of a thing is exalted, as much its multiplicity and separation decreased and weakens and its unity and cohesion becomes stronger.[42]

Viewpoint of Imam Khomeini

Imam Khomeini writes in this regard:

Beings slowly progress with the motion of perfection till they reach natural perfection in the bodily stage, which is the most moderate natural body. If it is observed that with regard to this gradual motion, insight and the eyes are opened to the world of Barzakh also. The last stage of the natural world and the first stage of the world of Barzakh and they don't consider the abstraction of Barzakh to be distinct, on the contrary he considers it to be the weakest stage and the other one as the stronger stage.

This same natural body (from the brain to the bones) day by day through the journey of perfection and by a motion from defectiveness to perfection reaches to a limit that it changes into a Barzakhi body. Although usually we are oblivious to the inner motion of our existence, therefore we imagine the world after death to be something distinct from the life of the world, oblivious of the fact that presently all the factors and capacities of divine power appointed as herders to take our capacity, body and natural life into the direction of the world and life of Barzakh and till now also remove us from the natural world. It is this same reasoning that you see throughout the life and gradually the flesh goes on decreasing, the eyes weaken day by day and the natural capacities continue to lose strength and the meaning of weakness and defect in nature is the changing of the natural body into the Barzakhi body. And it is the perfect stage of it. Our utmost is not aware of this change and transformation and in fact change and transformation of the proprietary into celestial is in the form of a force, and now all of our body in the condition that it is changed into a Barzakhi body –

---

[42] Asfar, Vol. 9, Part 2 of Fourth Journey, Part 4, Pg. 98

which is without matter. Like you see in dream that you are walking or eating or holding someone's hand; it is not only the amplitude of soul; on the contrary the body and hand that you see in the dream is the Barzakhi body and hand. It is mentioned in traditions that since some people deny Barzakh and the hereafter, the Almighty Allah gave them dreams so that it be a proof of that world.

The conclusion is that it is this same body, which is changed without its personality being deranged. It is not that after death, we are taken out from the worldly body and entered into a replica body, which was placed there. No, in reality in all the worlds, it is raised as one body and one fact and one personality. That is: when the excursion of its natural perfection is over and when all its natural capacities are changed into Barzakhi qualities, the natural body changes into a separate Barzakhi body. As if it has disposed of its skin and come out from the previous cover and since that previous covering was his own body at one time, it is necessary that his attachment to it should endure.[43]

Banu Ameen Isfahani writes in this regard:

The body of man is having two aspects: one is internal or hidden and the other is external or apparent. The external aspect is the same which has feelings and which is visible. And it is considered as a part of created things and events and is a specialty of this worldly constitution and it is worthy of enduring and permanent, because since the parts of this world continue forever to exist, spoil, change and transform, they do not remain in one condition forever, the apparent elemental body of man also (as mentioned in the third essay) continue forever to exist, spoil, change and transform, they do not remain in one condition forever and are always changing. It is that if we were not changing we would die and would be scattered from each other. This is matter is evident and does not need reasoning.

---

[43] Maad az Deedgah Imam Khomeini, Pg. 75

However his internal aspect, which in fact is the reality of this same body, and is considered to be part of man and his identity and without that the role and identity of man cannot be imagined. That is why a person perceives him by realization and not through his eyes and in no condition is he separated from it. So much so that even in sleep, he is not unaware of it.

It is correct that to scale the heights of perfection, our real soul in the beginning is needful of this elemental worldly body and beastly soul and for our satiation and formation in this world, which is one of the stages of perfection of man, on the contrary, our best excursion of perfection is a necessity in this world and we don't have any other causes.

We cannot but make use of them, and according to the necessity, we should maintain them as pure and healthy. And due to this we do not have the right to erase it, but we should know that our soul and reality, on the contrary the body with which our soul is associated, is other than this apparent body, which is visible and an instrument of the soul; because as we stated in the third essay – our knowledge develops connection with dimensions and apparent aspects of the things and not their reality and beings. And the reality of the body is that it is having the rank of the soul and the position of inner capacities of man. And anyone who refers to his own realization will nicely understand that he is a body whose soul is related to it even though in absence of eyes or other observational aspects, he may not know this physical constitution and apparent dimensions of his body as in the dream, when the eyes, ears all apparent senses of man are closed and the person understands himself through his inner realization; that he sees with the eyes and hears through the ears and in the same way all the parts of the body perform their functions, whereas others are unaware of his condition and they observe a motionless body and have no knowledge of his inner aspect. But in his dream, a man sees and feels everything as clearly as he sees in the waking world.

Compare the world of Barzakh to the world of dreams and know that the Almighty Allah has made the dreams and whatever is seen in dreams as examples of Barzakh, so that the imagination of the world of Barzakh becomes possible for us, even though the world of Barzakh with regard to this world is like awakening is to sleep.

In other words, the human body has two aspects: One is changeable, destructible and renewable and such that it never remains in the same form and cutting off its parts do not kill it. And another is permanent and everlasting; the first is the branch and the second is the root. The first is latitude and the second is essence. And as much as the soul scales the stages of perfection and becomes exalted, the real bodily aspect becomes cleaner, stronger and finer and its attachment to the soul increases and the unity between the spiritual and physical aspect becomes more intense and strong. Like you see so-and-so person dead and after some days his soul-less body decomposes. This skin and form is his real body and is considered as an happening and event of this natural world, which is always under change and transformation and which does not remain in the same form even for an hour, because this world is the world of being, decay, change and renewal.

When the lifespan of that man comes to an end and in the vessel of time with us he is not renewed and created, therefore the body, which was in the position of his dimensions and which had the necessity of endurance in incidentality and renewal; its aged parts wither away and are replaced by new parts. And when due to death he does not get new parts, necessarily his old parts decay and do not endure for another day in this world.

But that original essence is safe and the essence of life and that which was the abode of spiritual capacities, perceptive powers and activity of man remain with him. That essence is the reality of this worldly elemental body, which is the cause of the activity and identity of the soul and the soul by the command of he Lord initially becomes attached to it then using the apparent body passes the stages of perfection; but is dependant on it for its motion till it completes its excursion; and after that by the command of the Almighty that Barzakhi body is separated from this elemental body.[44]

Abode of Barzakh and Life in it

Barzakh implies distance between two things. The world of Barzakh is distance between this world; and the hereafter and final gathering.

Umar bin Yazid says: I asked Imam Ja'far Sadiq ('a): What is Barzakh? He replied: Barzakh begins from the time of death and burial in the grave and continues till Judgment Day.[45]

The man in his journey through creation has to cross a number of worlds. It is mentioned in the Holy Quran that:

"O man! surely you must strive (to attain) to your Lord, a hard striving until you meet Him."(84:6)

Hence the final destination of man is God, whereas this world is the tillage for the hereafter. The second journey is that of the grave and the world of Barzakh, which is to occur immediately after death without any time gap. The world of Barzakh is such that its inhabitants are not having a materiality, but they do have a body. They possess quantity, form, length and breadth etc. From the aspect of existence, it is a world, which is above and encompassing this world of nature. Life in Barzakh would be in accordance to the way a person lived in this world. The world of Barzakh is a world of abstractness, whose existence is proved

---

[44] Banu Ameen Isfahani, Maad Ya Aakhireen Saer-e-Bashar? Pg. 44
[45] Al-Kafi, Vol. 3, Pg. 242

in the neo-platonic philosophy. Therefore it would occur after this world and before the existence of abstract intellects and that is why it is called Barzakh. But it is necessary to note that this 'before-ness', 'after-ness' and 'middle-ness' is not of time and space; that it can be asked: Where is Barzakh? Is it located in this world or on some other planet or somewhere else? When has it come into existence or will come into existence? The reply is that time and space are signs of material things; while the fact is that Barzakh is a world, which is above the world and which encompasses it.

Human beings in the world of Barzakh have an opposite life: They enjoy some of the best bounties and spend their lives in happiness and comfort, but others are not same as far as the suffering of the punishment of Barzakh is concerned: Some are punished with the most severe punishment and some with lighter. In other words, the life of some is an example of the life of the hereafter and according to the interpretation of the traditions of the grave, it is a garden from the gardens of Paradise or it is a pit from the pits of Hell.

Aim of Punishment and Rewards of Barzakh

It is necessary to note that different bounties and punishments of Barzakh are shaped through beliefs, morals and deeds of man in the world. On the contrary, it is the good or bad deeds of man that assume the form of bounties and punishments of Barzakh as mentioned in verses of Quran and traditions:

The Holy Quran says:

> *"On the day that every soul shall find present what it has done of good and what it has done of evil, it shall wish that between it and that (evil) there were a long duration of time..."(3:30)*

And Allah says:

> **"(As for) those who swallow the property of the orphans unjustly, surely they only swallow fire into their bellies and they shall enter burning fire." (4:10)**

Amirul Momineen ('a) said:

"The deeds of people in the world would become visible to them in the hereafter."[46]

Imam Ja'far Sadiq ('a) said:

"When the dead body is placed in the grave, a person appears in it and says: We were three persons: your sustenance is over and the span of your life has ended. Your relatives have also abandoned you and gone away. I am your deeds and I would remain with you forever, but you considered me most unimportant in the world."[47]

Amirul Momineen ('a) said:

"On the last day of his worldly life and the first day of his entry into the world of the hereafter, man will see his wealth, children and deeds. Thus, he will address his wealth and say: 'I put myself into great hardships for your sake and was greedy. What help can you render to me today?' His wealth will reply: 'Take your burial shroud from me.' Then, he will address his children: 'I had been fond of you and throughout my life I took good care of you. What help can you render to me today?' They will reply: 'We will give you a proper burial.' Then, he will ask his deeds: 'I was shortcoming in observing you and you were difficult for me. What will do about me?' His deeds will reply: 'We will be there with you in the grave and on the Judgment Day till you are presented before your Lord.' Thus, if he is a friend of Allah

---

[46] Nahjul Balagha, Saying no. 7

[47] Biharul Anwar, Vol. 6, Pg. 265

(i.e. a believer), a fragrant, handsome and a well-dressed person will appear and say: 'Glad tidings to you of 'happiness and bounty' (Rooh wa Raihan) and Paradise. Blessed be your arrival. You are welcome!' The man will ask: 'Who are you?' He will be replied: 'I am your good deeds. I have come with you from the world and I will accompany you till Paradise.'"[48]

Perpetual Charity

As long as one is alive one is able to perform good deeds and practice the best of morals in order to make them as provisions for his life after death and that he may enjoy the hereafter. But by the occurrence of his death, the file of his deeds would be closed and he would be unable to do anything in the world.

But according to traditions, if man had performed the good deeds with regularity and with the intention of seeking divine proximity, he would enjoy their rewards after death in the world of Barzakh also. Some of those deeds are mentioned in traditions.

Imam Ja'far Sadiq ('a) said:

"There are six things whose rewards man would enjoy even after his death; a righteous son who prays for his salvation, the copy of Quran from which he used to read, a well which he had dug for public, trees that he had planted, canals of water that he had endowed as charity and the good practice, which he had established and which people continue to follow."[49]

Imam Ja'far Sadiq ('a) said:

"After death man is not rewarded except for one of the following three: A charity which he had founded; the reward of this charity will reach him till Judgment Day; a good custom that he has established,

---

[48] Al-Kafi, Vol. 3, Pg. 231

[49] Biharul Anwar, Vol. 6, Pg. 293

which is followed by others; and that he leaves a righteous son that prays for his salvation."[50]

The Messenger of Allah (s) said:

"When the believer dies, his deeds are over except three things: the charity left behind which continues after his death, a knowledge from which people benefit and a righteous son who prays for him."[51]

He also said: "When the believer dies leaving behind some knowledge (in writing); on Judgment Day those pages of knowledge would act as shields against the fire of Hell. And for each letter written in those pages, the Almighty Allah would bestow him a city seven times the size of this world."[52]

Abu Basir says: "I heard from Imam Ja'far Sadiq ('a) that he said:

One who teaches a good deed to someone would be rewarded equally as the one who is taught.

Abu Basir says: I asked the Imam: "What if the person who has learnt it, teaches it to others?"

He replied: The person to teach him first would be rewarded with the same rewards as all those who are subsequently taught it.

Abu Basir said: "What if the first person is dead?

He replied: Yes, even if he is dead.[53]

Imam Muhammad Baqir ('a) said:

"One who teaches a good deed to another would be rewarded equally as the one who is taught; without there being any decrease in the reward of the doer of the act. And one who teaches an evil deed to another, would be punished with the same punishment that the actual doer would be punished without there being any decrease in the punishment

---

[50] Biharul Anwar, Vol. 6, Pg. 293

[51] Biharul Anwar, Vol. 2, Pg. 22

[52] Biharul Anwar, Vol. 2, Pg. 144

[53] Biharul Anwar, Vol. 2, Pg. 17

of the one he has taught."[54]

Classes of Barzakh

There would be different kinds of people in Barzakh:

First group: Disbelievers and oppressors, who had no faith in the Almighty Allah, the Prophet and Resurrection during their life of the world. They considered themselves to be free and acted according to their whims and did not refrain from committing any evil. They would have a very hard life in Barzakh and they would be punished with different kinds of punishments. But they are nothing in comparison to the punishments of Hell.

Second group: Those who had faith in the Almighty Allah, the Prophet and Resurrection and who acted on their religious duties and refrained from prohibited acts. They would have a good life in Barzakh and would be bestowed with blessings, which would be a sample of the blessings reserved for them in Paradise.

Third group: Those who had faith in the Almighty Allah, the Prophet and Resurrection, and who performed their religious duties; but sometimes in carelessness they omitted an obligatory duty or committed unlawful act; but before death they repented for their sins and sought divine forgiveness; they would also not be punished in Barzakh.

Fourth group: Those who had faith in the Almighty Allah, the Prophet and Resurrection, and who performed their religious duties; but sometimes in carelessness they omitted an obligatory duty or committed unlawful act; but they died without repenting for their sins and seeking divine forgiveness. They would be punished in Barzakh in proportion to their sins and through it would be purified and on Judgment Day they would get the intercession of the Holy Prophet (s)

---

[54] Biharul Anwar, Vol. 2, Pg. 19

and the Holy Imams ('a) and they would be sent to Paradise after the accounting of the deeds.

Amr bin Yazid says: I asked Imam Ja'far Sadiq ('a): I have heard that you said:

All our Shias would go to Paradise?

He replied: "Yes, I said it and I am right; by Allah, all of them would enter Paradise."

The narrator asked: "May I be your ransom, even if they have numerous great sins to their credit?"

The Imam said: "As for the Judgment Day, all of you would enter Paradise through the intercession of the Prophet or his successor. But I am fearful about you with regard to Barzakh."

The narrator asked: "What is Barzakh?"

He replied: "It is there from the time of death and burial upto Judgment Day."[55]

Punishments of Barzakh

It is certain that there are different types of chastisements in Barzakh, but their exact quality is unknown to us. Since we are aware about the punishments and pleasures of the world and are not able to comprehend the matters of Barzakh and hereafter exactly as they are.

In some traditions, the world of Barzakh and its pleasures and hardships are compared different types of happy and terrifying dreams.

Sometimes in dream man sees different animals and stinging creatures and they attack him and he is pained due to their stings; he screams for help and due to the severity of discomfort perspires in profusion, while his body is in bed and has not suffered any damage. Sometimes he also sees pleasant and sweet dreams and he enjoys seeing them although his body derives no such enjoyment. Barzakh and the pleasures of man

---

[55] Biharul Anwar, Vol. 6, Pg. 267

in the world of Barzakh can be of such type.

It was inquired from Muhammad bin Ali ('a): "What is death?"

He replied:

"Death is the same sleep, which comes in search of you every night; with the difference that the duration of death is longer and you would not wake up till Judgment Day. Some people see dreams during sleep, which are extremely pleasing and so enjoyable that it is impossible to describe their pleasure. Others see terrifying matters, whose pain and discomfort is beyond computation. Thus what is the condition of pleasure and dread in a dream? Death is also like that; so prepare yourself for it."[56]

In this tradition, Barzakh is compared to sleep. Although with the important difference that Barzakh is not sleep; on the contrary with regard to the life of this world, it is a sort of awakening. Visions in the world of Barzakh are factual matters and it is from this aspect that feelings of pleasure and pain in them would also be extremely deeper and more lucid. Since in Barzakh, the connection between the soul and its material body is cut off, its memory and imagination becomes stronger. Its attention to the soul increases and it sees the good and bad qualities and its good and bad character inside its own being very clearly.

Bounties and Punishment of Barzakh

Mulla Mohsin Faiz Kashani has quoted from some scholars as follows:

One, who is attentive to his inner conscience in this world, would see that it is filled with different types of harmful and beastly things like lust, anger, deceit, jealousy, enmity, pride and selfishness.

These same qualities continue to attack and sting. Except that most people are deprived of this vision of their inner self since they are

---

[56] Biharul Anwar, Vol. 6, Pg. 155

involved in worldly matters and that which they can perceive through the senses. But when the curtain of unawareness is removed from the inner vision of man and he is placed in the grave, he would see them exactly and directly as personified in their appropriate forms. In the same condition, he sees that he is surrounded by scorpions and snakes and they are stinging him. In such a way that they are the same vices and bad qualities that he possessed in his inner self in the world and in Barzakh they have appeared in their real forms, because the inner matters possess their appropriate forms. And this is the punishment of a sinful person in the grave. The opposite circumstances would be there for one who has faith and is righteous.[57]

On another occasion, Faiz Kashani writes:

Pleasures and punishments related to the grave are not imaginary and lacking in an outward existence. Anyone who has such a belief is deviated. On the contrary, the matters of the grave, from the aspect of being are more powerful than the matters of worldly perception, because worldly forms in physical material are in the lowest stage of existence, whereas the form of existence in the grave, which are established for the soul of man, and as compared to worldly life, possess a more dignified existence and cannot be compared to worldly forms and in the same way, the two cannot be said to be same from the aspect of strength and weakness. In addition to this, both are perceptions of soul: one of them is perceived through the tools and physical strength and the other is felt through its own self; therefore it can be said: World and the hereafter are two conditions of the soul and that the make of the hereafter is in fact the exit of the soul from the filth and dust of physical form.[58]

---

[57] Faiz Kashani, Ilmul Yaqeen, Vol. 2, Pg. 883
[58] Faiz Kashani, Ilmul Yaqeen, Vol. 2, Pg. 889

An incident by Allamah Tabatabai

He says: A gnostic named Shaykh Abud lived in a corner of a room in the courtyard of the mausoleum of Amirul Momineen ('a) and he used to be occupied in his own circumstances. He rarely interacted with others and spent most of his time in worship and meditation. Sometimes he went to the Wadius Salam graveyard and spent hours there in meditation. When a dead body was brought for burial, he used to go to the grave and stare inside it. One day as he was returning from the graveyard, a person asked: Shaykh Abud, what is the news about Wadius Salam? He replied: No matter how much I searched in the graves, I could not find any snakes or scorpions; so I asked one of the graves: They say that you have snakes, scorpions and harmful creatures, but I don't see any such thing? The grave replied: We don't have snakes and scorpions, but it is the men who bring snakes and scorpions with them from the world.

Statement of Imam Khomeini

The Imam writes:

Man in the other world would not see the punishment except that which he has prepared in this world and he would see every good deeds, nice morals and correct beliefs; in that world he would see them with his own eyes, along with another blessing that God will bestow to him through His grace.

There is an ethereal and unseen form for each deed, whether good or bad, in the celestial world and the unseen sphere.[59]

---

[59] Maad az Deedgah Imam Khomeini, Pg. 333

Signs of the Judgment Day

The literal meaning of the Arabic word Qiyamah is something that happens all of a sudden. In the terminology of Quran, it is an important event that would occur at the end of the world and continue thereafter. All divine prophets and especially the Holy Prophet (s) have informed about this significant event. The Holy Quran has mentioned it in various terms. For example: Judgment Day, the Last Day, a day in which there is no relationship and friendship, the day on which all the people would be gathered, the day on which the people would be raised, the day of separation of the doers of good and evil, the day which would occur all of a sudden and so on. According to the Holy Quran the arrival of that day is absolutely imminent and it says: There is no doubt about it. But it has not mentioned the exact date of this event and has introduced it only as something, which would come all of a sudden. It can only be said that it would occur all of a sudden after the period of Barzakh is over. But as mentioned before, the world of Barzakh is contemporary to the period of this world and it is not bound by time and space. Since time and space are worldly phenomena, and Judgment Day is also after Barzakh; but this 'after-ness' is not the 'after-ness' of time and space, since in Qiyamat, the concepts of time and space would be cancelled and a new concepts would come into being; that is why the folks of Barzakh do not have proper awareness of the passage of time.

The Holy Quran says:

> *"And on the day when He will gather them as though they had not stayed but an hour of the day..." (10:45)*

And it also says:

> *"And at the time when the hour shall come, the guilty shall swear (that) they did not tarry but an hour..." (30:55)*

Although the Holy Quran has not mentioned the exact date of the occurrence of Qiyamat, it has indicated its signs.

Blowing of the Trumpet

One of the signs of Qiyamat is the blowing of the trumpet. According to Quran, at the end of the world, before the occurrence of Qiyamat, the trumpet would be blown twice and this important event is a sign that Qiyamat is near.

The Holy Quran says:

> *"And the trumpet shall be blown, so all those that are in the heavens and all those that are in the earth shall swoon, except such as Allah please; then it shall be blown again, then lo! they shall stand up awaiting." (39:68)*

The literal meaning of " is to become unconscious due to a terrifying heavenly scream and sometimes it brings death to the one who hears it according to the commentators who have interpreted this verse.

According to this verse, before Qiyamat the trumpet would be blown twice; on the first time, all the people present in the world would die and enter the world of Barzakh. And the second time all those who are in Barzakh would be enlivened and raised for Qiyamat.

In another verse, it is mentioned:

"And on the day when the trumpet shall be blown, then those who are in the heavens and those who are in the earth shall be terrified except such as Allah please, and all shall come to Him abased." (27:87)

According to this verse, before Qiyamat, the horn would be blown twice. The first time it would be to warn the people and prepare them for Qiyamat. During this first time all the inhabitants of the earth and the heavens would swoon due to its terror. But it is not mentioned that they would die. If the phrase 'those who are in the earth' implied those who are not dead yet, and who live in the earth, it should have mentioned: All would die at the first blowing and join those with the other folks of Barzakh, so that they may become ready for Qiyamat.

If it implies those who had died previously and who are present in Barzakh, but since they are still attached to worldly matters and are not able to forgo their attachment, and that is why it is possible to call them as 'those who are in the earth'; and it is also unlikely. Therefore it is necessary to consider the first blowing to be aimed at warning the people and making them ready for Qiyamat.

In the second blowing, by the natural command of the all-powerful Allah the system of matter and materiality would be destroyed and dismantled and the real exigencies of the system of cause and effect would become obvious. The inner aspects of man would become apparent. The reward and punishment of the deeds of man would be clear before the Almighty Allah and all this will not take more than a moment. The Almighty Allah says:

"(Of) the day when they shall come forth, nothing concerning them remains hidden to Allah. To whom belongs the kingdom this day? To Allah, the One, the Subduer (of all)."(40:16)

Yet another verse says:

"...and the trumpet will be blown, so We will gather them all together." (18:99)

On the basis of the above mentioned verses and other traditions, it can be said that the blowing of trumpet is imminent and that it is a sign of Qiyamat.

Now it should be seen what kind of a trumpet it is and how it would be blown? The dictionary meaning of 'trumpet' is something blown usually to make a public announcement or to warn the public about an impending invasion. In the past, this instrument was fashioned from animal horn, but it has evolved through the ages. Blowing the trumpet means creating a loud sound from it. Does the trumpet mentioned in the verse is in the same meaning and whether blowing into it should be interpreted as killing? Or it means something else?

With a little consideration, it would become clear that trumpet neither signifies the same particular instrument nor blowing of it can be said to be putting to death, because God is not a body that He should use a physical mean to make the living dead or to make them alive again.

The actions of the Almighty Allah are not like those of human beings that they should be in need of a tangible instrument.

The Almighty Allah is not in need of the blowing into a material tool in order to put to death the living or to enliven those who are dead. On the contrary, He does this through the angels appointed to capture the souls (Izrael) and angels appointed to enliven the dead.

Therefore, as Allamah Tabatabai has mentioned in the interpretation of the verse: Blowing of the trumpet is an allusion to a warning and the call for people to be present for Qiyamat.[60]

Other commentators have also interpreted this verse in the same way. A tradition of the Messenger of Allah (s) is used to support this contention. Sulaiman bin Arqam says: It has come down from the Holy Prophet (s) that when he was asked about the 'trumpet', he said that it was a horn (an instrument) of effulgence (Noor).[61]

In this tradition of the Messenger of Allah (s) the trumpet is a horn (an instrument) of effulgence (Noor). Therefore it does not have a material body like the horn or a metallic instrument; on the contrary it is a non-material medium for issuing a warning.

Collapse of the Solar System

One of the signs of Qiyamat is the collapse and complete derangement of the Solar System as mentioned in a number of verses of the Holy Quran. Some of them are as follows:

The Quran say:

> *"When the sun is covered, and when the stars darken, and when the mountains are made to pass away."(81:1-3)*

---

[60] Tafsirul Mizan, Vol. 14, Pg. 226

[61] Ibne Atiyya Andalusi, Al-Muharrarul Wajeez fee Kitabil Azeez, Vol. 5, Pg. 358; Asfar, Vol. 5, Pg.274; Faiz Kashani, Ilmul Yaqeen, Vol. 2, Pg. 891

"When the heaven becomes cleft asunder, and when the stars become dispersed, and when the seas are made to flow forth." (82:1-3)

"So when the stars are made to lose their light, and when the heaven is rent asunder, and when the mountains are carried away as dust." (77:8-10)

"On the day when the heaven shall move from side to side, and the mountains shall pass away passing away (altogether)." (52:9-10)

"When the great event comes to pass, there is no belying its coming to pass - abasing (one party), exalting (the other), when the earth shall be shaken with a (severe) shaking, and the mountains shall be made to crumble with (an awful) crumbling, so that they shall be as scattered dust." (56:1-6)

"On the day when We will roll up heaven like the rolling up of the scroll for writings..."(21:104)

"When the heaven bursts asunder, and obeys its Lord and it must. And when the earth is stretched, and casts forth what is in it and becomes empty, and obeys its Lord and it must."(84:1-5)

"He asks: When is the day of resurrection? So when the sight becomes dazed, and the moon becomes dark, and the sun and the moon are brought together." (75:6-9)

"And they ask you about the mountains. Say: My Lord will carry them away from the roots. Then leave it a plain, smooth level; You shall not see therein any crookedness or unevenness." (20:105-107)

"On the day when the earth shall be changed into a different earth, and the heavens (as well), and they shall come forth before Allah, the One, the Supreme." (14:48)

"Nay! when the earth is made to crumble to pieces..." (89:21)

"When the earth is shaken with her (violent) shaking, and the earth brings forth her burdens..." (99:1-2)

It can be concluded from such verses that very significant events would occur in this material world and there would be complete derangement in it. The heavens would split and merge into each other. The sun would lose its brilliance and heat and become dark. The moon would also darken. Stars would loose their sheen and be scattered in the atmosphere. Mountains would be rocked with tremors and shatter into particles. A terrible earthquake would rock the earth and all that is inside it would be expelled. The earth would sink into itself completely and would be changed into a completely new earth.

An important point: As mentioned previously with regard to the world of Barzakh, Qiyamat and total gatherings is an existing world, which would occur after the world of Barzakh; it is not in the breadth of this world or Barzakh; on the contrary with regard to the position of its existence it is along the length of the world of Barzakh and above it and encompassing it. Therefore it cannot be asked: When and where would Qiyamat occur?

Judgment Day in Quran

After the blowing of the trumpet and the death of all men; and the changing and sinking into themselves of the general systems of the earth and the heavens, the trumpet would be blown once again and all the human beings present in Barzakh would become alive again and present themselves before the Almighty Allah for accounting of their deeds.

The Holy Quran says:

> *"Do not these think that they shall be raised again, for a mighty day, the day on which men shall stand before the Lord of the worlds?" (83:4-6)*

According to the Holy Quran, the occurrence of Qiyamat is imminent and no one should have any doubt in it. It says:

> *"Allah, there is no god but He – He will most certainly gather you together on the resurrection day, there is no doubt in it;*

and who is more true in word than Allah?" (4:87)

Resurrection and life after death is a deep rooted belief as all divine prophets have informed about them. And most people throughout the ages, even in the pre-historic age, had believed in it. Although there are also some who have no faith in it. But they don't have any evidence to negate it; on the contrary they show its occurrence to be a doubtful matter.

The Quran says:

> *"And says man: What! when I am dead shall I truly be brought forth alive? Does not man remember that We created him before, when he was nothing?" (19:66-67)*

In reply to them and to negate its improbability, the Quran mentions the initial stage of the creation of man and says: We created man from a lifeless matter and then gave life to him. To enliven him a second time is obviously easier than the first creation and I have the power to do this. The following verses are clear evidences of it:

> *"He brings forth the living from the dead and brings forth the dead from the living, and gives life to the earth after its death, and thus shall you be brought forth."(30:19)*

> *"And He it is Who originates the creation, then reproduces it, and it is easy to Him..." (30:27)*

> *"O people! if you are in doubt about the raising, then surely*

We created you from dust, then from a small seed, then from a clot, then from a lump of flesh, complete in make and incomplete, that We may make clear to you; and We cause what We please to stay in the wombs till an appointed time, then We bring you forth as babies, then that you may attain your maturity; and of you is he who is caused to die, and of you is he who is brought back to the worst part of life, so that after having knowledge he does not know anything; and you see the earth sterile land, but when We send down on it the water, it stirs and swells and brings forth of every kind a beautiful herbage. This is because Allah is the Truth and because He gives life to the dead and because He has power over all things. And because the hour is coming, there is no doubt about it; and because Allah shall raise up those who are in the graves." (22:5-7)

The Holy Quran considers resurrection to be bodily and spiritual; common Muslims, on the contrary, followers of all heavenly religions have the same belief. That man would be raised on Judgment Day with the same personality and the same body that he had in this world. He would be raised in the same form and built as he had in the world and he would present himself before the Lord of the world.

In such a way that those who are acquainted with him would recognize him and remark: He is so and so person who was there in the world.

Most Muslims have consensus on the belief and it is also considered as a necessary principle of faith.

Allamah Majlisi has written in this connection:

All the believers in heavenly religions have consensus that resurrection would be bodily and it is a necessary principle of faith. Verses of Quran have very clearly explained this point and it is not right to interpret them in any other way. In addition to this an inordinate number of traditions (Mutawatir) prove the same.[62]

Sadruddin Shirazi writes:

The fact is that in resurrection, this same worldly body will return and not something like it; in such a way that if one sees that, he would say: He is so and so person that was present in the world.[63]

Faiz Kashani writes:

One who would come back in resurrection and one who would be herded in the hereafter, is the same human person that was present in the world and Barzakh, from the aspect of the soul as well as from the aspect of the body, in such a way that if someone sees him in the field of gathering, he would say: He is so and so person that was present in the world. As Imam Ja'far Sadiq ('a) said with regard to Barzakh: If you see him, you would say: He is that same so and so person that was present in the world.[64]

Therefore we should accept that the man who would be herded in Qiyamat is the same person from the aspect of the soul as well as the body, who lived in the world with the important difference that the body of the world was subject to change, it was prone to disease and old age; but on the contrary the form of the hereafter does not age and is not prone to disease.

The Messenger of Allah (s) said:

O children of Abdul Muttalib, the guards do not lie to their folks. By Allah, you will die just as you go to sleep and just as you awake from sleep, you would also be raised up after death.

After death, there is nothing except Paradise or Hell and the creation and raising of people for Qiyamat is just like the creation of a single

---

[62] Biharul Anwar, Vol. 7, Pg. 47

[63] Al-Mubda wal Maad, Pg. 490

[64] Ilmul Yaqeen, Vol. 2, Pg. 902

person and not more than that. The Almighty Allah says in the Holy Quran:

"Neither your creation nor your raising is anything but as a single soul..." (31:28)[65]

Imam Muhammad Baqir ('a) said:

Luqman said to his son: My son, if you have doubt about death, you should try not to go to sleep; and see that you would not be able to do that. And if you have doubt about the raising in Qiyamat, try not to wake up; and you will not be able to do that. If you think upon this, you would understand that your soul is in the control of someone else. Indeed, sleep is like death and waking up from sleep is like raising after death.[66]

---

[65] Biharul Anwar, Vol. 7, Pg. 47

[66] Biharul Anwar, Vol. 7, Pg. 42

Gathering of humans (Hashr)

In some traditions, it has come that human beings would assemble in Qiyamat in various forms. Mu'adh bin Jabal asked the Messenger of Allah (s) about the interpretation of the verse of Quran that reads:

> "The day on which the trumpet shall be blown so you shall come forth in hosts." (78:18)

The Messenger of Allah (s) said:
You have asked about an extremely great matter!
Then, with tearful eyes, he said:
Ten groups from my Ummah would be distinguished from others and they would be gathered in different forms: some would come in form of monkeys and pigs in Qiyamat. Some would be brought upside down; they would be dragging their shoulders. Some would be presented blind and they would also walk in the same way. Some would be brought deaf and dumb and they would not understand anything. Some would

come chewing their tongues while it would be hanging on their chests and blood and puss would be flowing from their mouths and the folks of the gathering would be disgusted with them.

Some would have their limbs cut off. Some would be crucified on branches of fire. Some would stink more than carrion. Some would be dressed in clothes that would be dyed in tar and it would be sticking to their bodies.

Those who would be brought in the form of monkeys are actually those who spread mischief through lies and rumors. Those who would be brought in the form of pigs would be those who made money through unlawful means. Those who move on their faces would be those took usury. Those who would be brought deaf and dumb would be those who were conceited.

Those chewing their tongues would in fact be religious scholars and judges, whose actions were opposed to their words.

Those who would have their limbs cut off would be those who had harassed their neighbors.

Those who hung from branches of fire would be those who spy on others.

Those stinking more than carrion would be those who followed the unlawful carnal desires and who did not pay the share of Allah and the poor from their wealth.

Those who would come with their clothes smeared in tar would be the conceited and arrogant ones.[67]

The Messenger of Allah (s) said:

The proud would be brought on Judgment Day in the form of small ants and they would be trampled by the folks of gathering till the accounting of the people is over.[68]

---

[67] Jalaluddin Suyuti, Durre Manthur, Vol. 8, Pg. 393

[68] Wasailush Shia, Vol. 15, Pg. 379

The Messenger of Allah (s) also said:

One who cheats Muslims in trade is not from us (a Muslim) and on Judgment Day he would be raised with the Jews, since they were also habitual cheaters.[69]

From the abovementioned traditions and tens of other such reports, it can be concluded that some people would be raised on Judgment Day in the form of animals. It is said that it does not imply that their form and worldly body would be changed into the form and worldly body of animals, as it was previously stated that man after death would come in Barzakh and Qiyamat with the same body that he possessed in the world. In such a way that whoever sees him would remark: It is the same so and so person who was there in the world. On the contrary, it implies that the being of such persons would change into the being of animal and they would really be brought as animals.

Even though their forms would be human, since in the world the animal manners and powers have completely dominated them, internally they have turned into animals, but others would be unaware of this; but since Judgment Day is the day when the inner being of man would be exposed, their being animals would also become apparent, although they would be there in human forms, since there is beastliness of animals in their beings and not in form or make-up.

Imam Khomeini has said with regard to this:

Just as man is having a particular worldly form in this world…there is a particular form for him, which is unseen, whose form is under the control of self and inner being in the world after death, whether it be Barzakh or Qiyamat. If the inner and secret being of man is human, his spiritual form is also human. But if it is non-human, his form is also not human. For example, if carnal and beastly desires dominate his inner self and the inner being becomes a beast, man is a beast in the form of

---

[69] Wasailush Shia, Vol. 17, Pg. 383

a celestial entity according to that creation. And if feeling of anger and ferocity dominates his inner being, that fierceness would become his unseen celestial form. And if doubts and satanity become dominant and his inner being assumes satanic inclinations like deception, dishonesty, lying, back biting, his unseen and ethereal form is that of one of the satans, depending on the evil quality affecting him.[70]

---

[70] Maad az Deedgah Imam Khomeini, Pg. 354

Scroll of deeds

It can be concluded from verses of Quran and traditions that all good and bad deeds, words, beliefs and views of man are recorded in a scroll by the angels appointed on him by the Almighty Allah. The Holy Quran says:

> *"And most surely there are keepers over you. Honorable recorders, they know what you do."(82:10-12)*

That writing in the terminology of Quran is named as 'bird' and 'book'. It is also said in Quran that:

> *"And We have made every man's actions to cling to his neck, and We will bring forth to him on the resurrection day a book which he will find wide open: Read your book; your own self is sufficient as a reckoner against you this day."* (17:13-14)

Raghib Isfahani has interpreted 'bird' as good and bad deeds, which a person performs or commits.[71]

According to verses of Quran, angels appointed by Allah on each man make two scrolls: scroll of good deeds and scroll of evil deeds. Scrolls related to him would be hung from his neck, so that on Judgment Day he may read it and become aware of his character.

'Book' implies a written thing. Writing in general parlance among us is interpreted as inscribing of letters, words and sentences, which prove a particular meaning according to social consonance inscribed on sheets of paper or any other tablet, which is capable to preserve those inscriptions. So that in future he can read it himself and other who are aware of the situation may also know what is written therein. But in any case, the reasoning of these writings and words is nominal and conventional and not actual or real.

Now the question that arises is that whether the writing of angels and preparation of the scroll of deeds from human beings is also of the same kind or some other kind? Would they rely on these same writings of lines and pictures? Would all these deeds be written on sheets of paper or other tablets? And would these be hung from necks of people, so that they may remain till Judgment Day? Such a supposition is basically unimaginable. Apart from this, it is not compatible with the contents of some Quranic verses, since it is concluded from verses and traditions that in Qiyamat, man would see his actual good and bad deeds and not their written records.

The Almighty Allah says in the Holy Quran:

"On the day that every soul shall find present what it has done of good and what it has done of evil, it shall wish that

---

[71] Mufradat, under the term 'Tayr'

between it and that (evil) there were a long duration of time; and Allah makes you to be cautious of (retribution from) Himself; and Allah is Compassionate to the servants." (3:30)

And He also says:

"And the Book shall be placed, then you will see the guilty fearing from what is in it, and they will say: Ah! woe to us! what a book is this! it does not omit a small one nor a great one, but numbers them (all); and what they had done they shall find present (there); and your Lord does not deal unjustly with anyone." (18:49)

Many important points can be concluded from these verses:

1. In Qiyamat, the actual good and bad deeds of man would be presented before him and he would observe them and not a record of them.

2. The bad character of man (which was in his conscience) would not be separated from him and a desire to be separated from it would be useless.

3. All the good and bad deeds of man would be recorded in the scroll of deeds and even the smallest act would not be missed. He would see them (gathered) at a single place and would be astounded by it.

The same meaning is intended in some traditions.

Abul Jarud has narrated from Imam Muhammad Baqir ('a) that he said in the interpretation of the verse:

"And We have made every man's actions to cling to his neck...

"*(17:13)*

The Imam said:

The good and bad deeds of man would accompany him and it would not be possible to be separated from them, till the scroll of his deeds is given to him in Qiyamat.[72]

Khalid bin Najih has narrated from Imam Ja'far Sadiq ('a) that he said:

When the Judgment Day would be established, the scroll of deeds of every man would be given to him. At that time he would be told: Read your book.

The narrator asked: Does he know what is written therein?

Imam ('a) replied:

The Almighty Allah would remind him of every act. Thus he would remember whatever he had done all through his life, even though it might be in the blink of an eye, or a word that he spoke or a step that he took; as if he has committed it that very moment.

Therefore the Quran says:

"Ah! woe to us! what a book is this! it does not omit a small one nor a great one, but numbers them (all)..." (18:49)[73]

Amirul Momineen ('a) said:

On the last day of his worldly life and the first day of his entry into the world of the hereafter, the man would see his wealth, children and deeds. Thus he would address his wealth and say: I put myself into great hardships for your sake and was greedy; what help can you render to me today? His wealth would reply: Take your burial shroud from

---

[72] Biharul Anwar, Vol. 7, Pg. 312

[73] Biharul Anwar, Vol. 7, Pg. 315

me. Then he would address his children: I had been fond of you and throughout my life, I took good care of you; what help can you render to me today? They would reply: We would give you a proper burial. Then he would ask his deeds: I was shortcoming in observing you and you were difficult for me; what will you do about me?

His deeds would reply: I would be there with you in the grave and on the Judgment Day, till you are presented before your Lord. Thus if he is a believer, a fragrant, handsome and a well-dressed person would appear and say: Glad tidings to you of 'happiness and bounty' (Rooh wa Raihan) and Paradise. Blessed be your arrival; you are welcome! The dead man would ask: Who are you? He replies: I am your good deeds. I have come with from the world and I would accompany you till Paradise."[74]

Therefore, true and false beliefs, good and bad morals, good and bad character are present in the inner being of man in this world also but due to worldly preoccupations, he is unaware of their existence. But in Qiyamat, when the curtain would be removed from his conscience, he would find all of them with himself at one and the same time. He would exclaim due to this astounding phenomenon and he would be told: Just as you were unaware of this matter in the world, We removed the curtain from your eyes and today your eyesight has become very sharp.[75]

At this point, a question arises that the good and bad actions and words of man in the world are transient; that is they occur and then pass away; how can it be imagined that they would remain till Judgment Day? For example Prayer consists of Takbiratul Ihram, recitation of Surah Hamd and another Surah, genuflection and prostration, Tashahud and salutation and all of them are transient phenomena, and they cannot

---

[74] Al-Kafi, Vol. 3, Pg. 231

[75] Ilmul Yaqeen, Vol. 2, Pg. 938

remain forever; all the good and bad deeds are of the same kind.

It is better that to solve this difficulty through the statements of a scholar who is well versed with this subject. He writes:

Everything a sane person can understand through his senses would leave an imprint on his soul and it would be stored in the treasure-trove of his perceptions. In the same way, every good or bad deed that he commits, no matter how small it is, its effect is recorded in the scroll of the soul; especially the acts, which become a habit and a second nature as a result of repetition. He same nature would lead one to either remain in Paradise or Hell forever. Since the carnal habits change into an elemental form that they affect the invention of spiritual bounties and punishments. If the effect of acts and words on the soul had not been permanent and lasting, and do not intensify gradually in such a way that they become a part of that person's nature, no one would have been able to master any art. Punishment, discipline, training and education of children would also have been useless. And it would have made man same from the time of his childhood till the end of his life and no difference would have been possible. In that case, religious duties (for purification and training of the soul) would be useless and absurd.

And if habits had no permanence and essence and they had not been everlasting, the enduring of the people of Paradise in bounties and the living of the folks of Hell in punishment forever would have been absurd.

If the source of reward and punishment had been the deeds of man themselves, in the circumstances that actions and words are destroyed, it would necessitate that the effect would remain without the presence of the cause; and this is not correct. Physical action, which occurred in a limited time, how can it be the source of everlasting recompense?

Such justifications do not befit the Almighty Allah.[76]

Statement of Imam Khomeini

With regard to this, the Imam writes:

Intention is the practical form and the celestial aspect of the act. And in the holy traditions same point is mentioned when it is said: Intention is superior to action; on the contrary intention is action itself. And this is not an exaggeration as some have suggested, it is a fact, because intention is the perfect form of the act and a part of its whole; and health and decay, perfection and defects of the acts is with regard to it only. Hence an act through the medium of intention is sometimes an honor and sometimes it is disrespect; sometimes it is perfection and sometimes it is defectiveness. Sometimes it is of the high celestial kind in a beautiful form and sometimes it is from the lowest level and in a horrific form.[77]

---

[76] Ilmul Yaqeen, Vol. 2, Pg. 938

[77] Maad az Deedgah Imam Khomeini, Pg. 339

Scale of deeds

According to verse of Quran and traditions of the Infallibles, it can be concluded that in Qiyamat, a scale would be established in order to weigh the good and bad deeds of people. Weighing of deeds is an Islamic principle and it is a part of accounting.

The Quran says:

"And We will set up a just balance on the day of resurrection, so no soul shall be dealt with unjustly in the least; and though there be the weight of a grain of mustard seed, (yet) will We bring it, and sufficient are We to take account." (21:47)

Balance (Mizan) is an instrument of fixing the quantity of goods and commodities. This instrument has been common in different nations and communities in various forms, although mostly it is constructed from tangible materials and bodies are weighed through it, but it is not restricted only to material affairs; on the contrary in reality it is used in other matters as well.

The science of logic used to discriminate between right and wrong judgment, is also called as the 'science of balance'. In the exposition of the quantum of consciousness, memory, sciences, information, people use the written and oral experiments and name them as 'balance of exposing the reality', and other matters of this type. Therefore the implication of 'balance' does necessarily have to be something material.

Since the balance of Qiyamat is also same, because it is a medium to identify faith and principles of belief, good and bad morals, righteous and evils deeds, it cannot be a worldly and a physical matter.

Can prayer, fasting, sincerity, piety, faith, truthfulness, trustworthiness be weighed on a worldly balance?

A person asked Imam Ja'far Sadiq ('a): "Would the deeds of people not be weighed in Qiyamat?"

He replied:

"No, since deeds have no body; that which would be weighed in the balance would be its quality (effect). One who wants to find the weight or quantity of something needs a balance. While the fact is that nothing is hidden from the Almighty Allah."

So, the person asked: "Then what is the meaning of the weighing of deeds?"

The Imam said:

"That is justice would be observed in accounting and recompense of deeds."

He asked, "Then what is the meaning of the verse:

"...Then as for him whose measure (of good deeds) is heavy..."
(7:8)

He replied:

"It means that his good deeds would be more."[78]

Therefore the balance of deeds in Qiyamat is not like the usual balances, which have a worldly body; on the contrary it should be of another kind. It is possible to choose between two causes in the interpretation of balance in Qiyamat:

First reason: It is that balance consists of correct beliefs, ethical values and laws of the Shariat, which are in fact the straight path, wayfaring on the path of Allah and attainment of the lofty stages of humanity. Therefore, in Qiyamat, the deeds of every man would be weighed on the criterion of Shariat and rewarded accordingly. The same point is indicated in traditions:

The Messenger of Allah (s) said:

"Justice is the balance of God on the earth, one who acts on it would be admitted in Paradise and one who leaves it, would be thrown into Hell."[78]

Imam Ja'far Sadiq ('a) said:

"One who recites the formula of 'there is no god except Allah,' with sincerity would be admitted in Paradise and sincerity lies in the fact that the testimony of 'there is no god except Allah,' should prevent him from committing of prohibited acts."[79]

The Messenger of Allah (s) said:

"Prayer is the balance; one who fulfills its rights would be recompensed completely."[80]

The Messenger of Allah (s) said:

"Nothing is placed in the balance of deeds of the people in Qiyamat, which is superior to good behavior."[81]

---

[78] Biharul Anwar, Vol. 7, Pg. 248

[79] Wasailush Shia, Vol. 15, Pg. 257

[80] Kafi, Vol. 3, Pg. 268

[81] Kafi, Vol. 2, Pg. 100

Imam Ja'far Sadiq ('a) said:

"One who meets the Almighty Allah with the following ten things would be admitted to Paradise: Testimony of 'there is no god but Allah,'; testimony that Muhammad is the Messenger of Allah; confession of all that has come from the Almighty Allah; establishing of prayer; paying of Zakat; fasting in the month of Ramadhan; Hajj of the Holy Kaaba; acceptance of the guardianship (Wilayat) of the holy personalities (Awliya) of Allah; immunity from enemies of Allah and refraining from alcohol."[82]

Second reason: It is that balance of deeds is in fact the holy reflection of deeds and views of prophets and infallible Imams. Since these holy personalities are guides of humanity, they themselves acted in accordance to laws of Shariat and practiced the best of morals in such a way that perfections of humanity were personified in them. They also called the people to same beliefs and morals. Hence all beliefs, acts, morals and traits of character can be judged on their criterion; thus they are considered to be the balance of deeds. The same interpretation is mentioned in some traditional reports.

Imam Ja'far Sadiq ('a) said in the interpretation of the verse:

"And We will set up a just balance on the day of resurrection..."(21:47)

"They are the prophets and their successors."[83]

Imam Sajjad ('a) said:

"Ali ('a) is the chief of faith and the balance of deeds."[84]

---

[82] Wasailush Shia, Vol. 1, Pg. 30

[83] Kafi, Vol. 1, Pg. 420

[84] Mustadrakul Wasail, Vol. 10, Pg. 224

Imam Ja'far Sadiq ('a) said:

"By Allah, Ali is the straight path and the balance of deeds."[85]

The Messenger of Allah (s) said:

"I am the balance of knowledge and Ali is the two pans of balance, Hasan and Husain are its cords and Fatima is the connecting rod between them and the Imams after Hasan and Husain would be the criterion of recognition of their friends and their enemies."[86]

Therefore the holy beings of prophets and their infallible successors can also be interpreted as the balance to weigh the deeds of the people of the community, but think upon it for a moment and you will see that that the second reason also returns to the first cause, since the beings of the prophets and successors are personification of beliefs, morals and good character of religion, they are introduced as balance; thus the balance is in fact a criterion to weigh beliefs and deeds and laws of religion. And the deeds of every person can be weighed in it and he could be rewarded and punished accordingly. In this weighing, beliefs and deeds of a person would be placed in one pan and the other pan contains all beliefs, morals and laws of religion.

From some verses of Quran it can be concluded that man has not one, but many balances.

> *"And the measuring out on that day will be just; then as for him whose measure (of good deeds) is heavy, those are they who shall be successful. And as for him whose measure (of good deeds) is light, those are they who have made their souls suffer loss because they disbelieved in Our communications." (7:8-9)*

---

[85] Biharul Anwar, Vol. 35, Pg. 343

[86] Biharul Anwar, Vol. 23, Pg. 107

In this verse, the point mentioned is about the heaviness of the balances of some people and the lightness of the balances of others. It can be concluded that every person would have a number of balances. Perhaps it would be from the aspect that the beliefs would be weighed in one balance, while morals would be weighed in another and deeds would be weighed in yet another balance; thus if each belief is weighed against the correct belief, and every deed is weighed against proper deeds and every moral is weighed against right morals all in different balances, each person would have a number of balances.

Process of weighing the deeds

The background of the heaviness and lightness of the pan of balance is obtained in this world through beliefs, morals, character and speech of man: correct beliefs make the self illuminated, and one who has a stronger faith has more illuminated self. Even though good morals and nice manners are also of the same sort, good deeds, worship and other charitable acts are accidental and they do not endure, but through sincerity and good intention assume the form of a second nature and illuminate and polish the self of man and strengthen his human aspects and make the pan of his deeds heavier.

On the other hand, false beliefs, morals and evil deeds make the soul dark and terrifying; his aspect of humanity is weakened and the aspect of his bestiality is strengthened and so much so that sometimes in his inner being, he assumes the form of a carnivorous beast and the pan of his humanity becomes light.

All these acts, reactions and changes occur in this world and inside the self, but he himself is unaware of them, till on Judgment Day the curtain would be removed from his eyes.

"On the day when hidden things shall be made manifest."

(86:9)

He would see all of them with his own eyes. At that time he would find the pan of balance of his self either light or heavy.

Accounting of deeds

According to verses of Quran and traditions of the holy infallibles ('a), the accounting of deeds is an imminent and a necessary matter. Although in Qiyamat, every person would be having his scroll of deeds with him, in which everything is recorded, but since his deeds throughout the life were widespread and he does not have complete awareness about them, in Qiyamat, in the presence of the Almighty Allah he would be presented with them, so that he may observe them with his own eyes.

In the Holy Quran it is mentioned that:

> *"On that day men shall come forth in sundry bodies that they may be shown their works. So he who has done an atom's weight of good shall see it. And he who has done an atom's weight of evil shall see it." (99:6-8)*

And it also says:

> *"On the day that every soul shall find present what it has done of good and what it has done of evil, it shall wish that between it and that (evil) there were a long duration of time..."(3:30)*

In Qiyamat and with the accounting of deeds, the scroll of deeds of every man would be handed over to him, but all the people would not get their scroll in the same manner. On the contrary the scroll of the believers and righteous would be given to them in their right hands and this is a sign of their easy accounting. And the scroll of infidels and oppressors would be given behind the head and in the left hand, which is a sign of difficulty in accounting.

The Holy Quran says:

> *"Then as to him who is given his book in his right hand. He shall be reckoned with by an easy reckoning. And he shall go back to his people joyful. And as to him who is given his book behind his back. He shall call for perdition. And enter into burning fire." (84:7-12)*

Kinds of people on Judgment Day

There would be three types of people on Judgment Day:

1. The Righteous: It is the group of those who have the highest ranks from the aspect of faith and good deeds; they followed the Shariat to perfection and did not commit anything unlawful. There would be no accounting of such people and they would be sent to Paradise before all.

The Holy Quran says:

> *"And at the time when the hour shall come, at that time they*

shall become separated one from the other. Then as to those who believed and did good, they shall be made happy in a garden." (30:14-15)

And it also says:

"And you shall be three sorts. Then (as to) the companions of the right hand; how happy are the companions of the right hand! And (as to) the companions of the left hand; how wretched are the companions of the left hand! And the foremost are the foremost. These are they who are drawn nigh (to Allah)." (56:7-11)

Allamah Tabatabai has written in the interpretation of this verse that: The 'foremost' in the verse are those who took precedence over others in performing good deeds and from this aspect they have precedence over others in getting salvation and mercy of the Almighty Allah.[87]

Polytheists, infidels and oppressors: This group also would be shocked in Qiyamat by looking at their scroll of deeds, which would be dark and full of evil, corruptions and harmful habits and would not see any light either in themselves and their scroll of deeds, they would find themselves in complete loss. Their fate is obvious and there is no need of any accounting. They have no good deed to their credit that there should be a need to account them, since faith is necessary for acceptance of deeds.

The Holy Quran says:

---

[87] Al-Mizan, Vol. 19, Pg. 117

> "And as to those who disbelieved and rejected Our communications and the meeting of the hereafter, these shall be brought over to the chastisement." (30:16)

And it also says:

> "Then it shall be said to those who were unjust: Taste abiding chastisement; you are not requited except for what you earned." (10:52)

And it also says:

> "...And whoever disbelieves in the communications of Allah then surely Allah is quick in reckoning." (3:19)

And further says:

> "And (as for) those who disbelieve, their deeds are like the mirage in a desert, which the thirsty man deems to be water; until when he comes to it he finds it to be naught, and there he finds Allah, so He pays back to him his reckoning in full; and Allah is quick in reckoning."(24:39)

And then says:

> "Surely Allah does not forgive that anything should be associated with Him..."(4:48)

Imam Sajjad ('a) has said in a lengthy tradition:

"No balance would be fixed for the polytheists and no scroll would be unfurled; the unfurling of the scroll is only for the Muslims."[88]

The Messenger of Allah (s) said:

"Allah, the Mighty and Sublime takes the accounts of the deeds of all the people except those who were polytheists; no accounting would be there for such people and they would be thrown into Hell right away."[89]

3. In the middle: The third group would be of those who were neither complete disbelievers nor sincere believers; on the contrary they were in the middle; but they had faith in Allah, in the Prophet and in resurrection and they performed their duties according to their ability and have good deeds to their credit. But as a result of the weakness of their faith they also have some shortcomings and defects. The Quran says:

"And others have confessed their faults, they have mingled a good deed and an evil one; may be Allah will turn to them (mercifully); surely Allah is Forgiving, Merciful." (9:102)

Accounting is needed for the determination of the final destiny of these people. Although the fact is that the Almighty Allah is fully aware of the deeds of people and even the smallest point is not hidden from Him, and everything is clear to Him even before the accounting and He is also cognizant of the final consequence of everything; in spite of that the accounting of deeds on Judgment Day is a necessary matter. It is so because man forgets whatever good or bad he has done throughout his life. Moreover he only sees the apparent aspect of his deeds and is unaware of the hidden aspects and that is why he expects rewards for which he is not eligible. The Almighty Allah rewards and punishes

---

[88] Biharul Anwar, Vol. 7, Pg. 259

[89] Biharul Anwar, Vol. 7, Pg. 260

people according to the eligibility of the person and not on the basis of his expectations. That is why the accounting of Judgment Day is necessary, so that people should not have any excuse and that they should know that they have been dealt with justice.

The accounting of Judgment Day is very detailed and accurate and everything would be questioned. Here we shall mention some of them in brief to illustrate our assertion:

Matters that would be questioned in Qiyamat

First: Principles of belief: The first and the most important matter that would be subject to inquiry are the principles of faith. Beliefs from different aspects would be adjudged and evaluated; did he have faith in all of them or he was in doubt about some of them or denied them? Were the people sincere about them or their beliefs were stained with some nonsensical matter? Were the principles of faith deeply rooted in his being or they did not cross the limit of verbal expression and imagination? Such matters are effective in the perfection of the spiritual light and ranks of men in the hereafter and they would become clear in Qiyamat and at the time of accounting.

First: Blessings: Blessings that the Almighty Allah has bestowed to His servants to serve as venture capital of worldly trade and a medium of obtaining provisions for the hereafter. On Judgment Day and during the accounting all valuable blessings would be asked about. The world is really tillage of the hereafter and the business place of mankind.

The Messenger of Allah (s) said:

"The world is the agricultural field of the hereafter."[90]

Amirul Momineen ('a) said:

"For the righteous believers in the Almighty Allah, the world is a trading house; they earn the mercy of Allah in it; and they gain Paradise

---

[90] Ibne Abil Jamhur Ahsai, Awaliul Layali

as profits."[91]

The valuable bounties of the Almighty Allah are so numerous that a number of traditions have mentioned that they would be asked about on Judgment Day.

The Messenger of Allah (s) said:

"On Judgment Day, man would not be able to take a single step without being questioned about some things. His age, how he spent it? His youth, how he used it? His wealth, how he earned it and where he spent it? And love and affection for us, Ahle Bayt."[92]

The Holy Prophet (s) said in another tradition:

"Everyday, twenty-four treasures would be opened up for man in Qiyamat equal to the hours in a day. When he sees the treasures, which would be full of light and pleasure, he would be so pleased that if his happiness is distributed among all the folks of Hell, they would forget the chastisements of Hell. That treasure is related to the hour in which he worshipped the Almighty Allah. At that time, another treasure would be opened for him, which would be dark and terrifying. He would scream on seeing that with such terror that if the same terror is distributed among all the folks of Paradise they would forget the pleasures of Paradise. It is the hour when he was involved in disobedience of the Almighty Allah. Then another treasure would be opened for him in which he would not be able to see anything as it is related to the time when he was asleep or involved in some lawful worldly activities; on seeing that he would feel regret that he did not utilize it for some profitable deed; he would regret it so deeply that it cannot be described. That is why the Judgment Day is also called as the 'day of loss and gain.'"[93]

---

[91] Biharul Anwar, Vol. 70, Pg. 100

[92] Biharul Anwar, Vol. 70, Pg. 258

[93] Biharul Anwar, Vol. 70, Pg. 273

Third: Worship acts: Obligatory and recommended acts like prayer, fasting, Hajj, supplication, charities and other worship acts would be accepted and rewarded only if they fulfill the following conditions: Firstly: They should be performed according to the criterion of religious laws as ordered by the Prophet. Secondly: They should have been performed seeking the pleasure of Allah and His proximity. If they were done to show-off or time pass; not only would they go unrewarded, on the contrary they would be considered as a kind of polytheism.

Imam Ja'far Sadiq ('a) said:

"Every act performed for show-off is polytheism. One, who does something for someone other than Allah, should seek the reward of the same from that person only; and one who does something for the Almighty Allah, his reward is upon the Almighty Allah."[94]

Ali bin Salim says: I heard Imam Ja'far Sadiq ('a) say:

"The Almighty Allah has said: I am the best partner; I will not accept the deed of anyone who makes something other than Me as his partner. I only accept the deed performed for Me exclusively."[95]

How numerous are those who spend years in worship and are pleased by it and imagine themselves to be deserving of Paradise, others also consider them to be such, but since they were for something or someone other than Allah, in Qiyamat and after accounting of deeds, they would not be rewarded. God forbid!

Fourth: Everlasting philanthropy: Charities and public welfare projects that require funds like Hajj, Umrah, Ziyarat, construction of Masjids, hospitals, clinics, schools, universities and other philanthropic activities, which are called as everlasting charities; such activities would be greatly valuable, but subject to two conditions: First is that they should have been performed with the intention of gaining proximity

---

[94] Kafi, Vol. 2, Pg. 293

[95] Kafi, Vol. 2, Pg. 295

to Almighty Allah and not for fame, name or social status as mentioned earlier. The second condition is that the money spent should be lawful; otherwise it would be of no use in Qiyamat.

Imam Ja'far Sadiq ('a) said:

"If someone obtains money through illegal means and with that money goes for Hajj, when he recites the Thalbiya (Labbaik) at the time of putting on the Ihram dress, he would be told by Almighty Allah: 'Neither I accept nor do I welcome you'; but when the expenses of Hajj are paid through lawful funds, at the time of Thalbiya he would be told: 'I accept you and welcome you.'"[96]

The Messenger of Allah (s) said:

"If man has earned money through unlawful means, and he spends in charity from it, he would not get any reward for it; and if he spends it in his life, it would not be blessed. And if he leaves it in inheritance, it would be a provision for the fire of Hell."[97]

How numerous are those who form charities and are considered righteous and are pleased at this and also consider themselves eligible for enormous divine rewards. But since it was all through unlawful money, there would be no reward for them in the hereafter. All this would become clear on Judgment Day after the accounting.

Most Difficult Stages of Accounting

The most difficult stages of accounting are concerned with oppressing people and with the mutual rights of men. People live with each other and have rights on each other. To fulfill the rights of each other is a religious duty of man. The prophets and the Holy Prophet (S) has emphasized on this matter that in Qiyamat they would have to account for them particularly.

The rights of people are numerous. Each of them is named and its

---

[96] Wasailush Shia, Vol. 17, Pg. 89

[97] Biharul Anwar, Vol. 103, Pg. 14

details are given in books of traditions and here it is not necessary to mention all of them fully and neither is it possible to do so.

We shall mention only some of them in brief: every married couple, parents and children, relatives, neighbors and fellow citizens, youths and aged, teachers and students, wealthy and poor, agents and subordinates, co-religionists and fellow countrymen...have mutual rights and duties on each other and their fulfillment is a moral, religious and social duty. And to violate them is considered a sin and a crime, which would be accounted for in Qiyamat.

It is possible that in Qiyamat the Almighty Allah may overlook violation of His rights, but He will not overlook the violation of the rights of people, except if those whose rights have been violated permit it.

Amirul Momineen ('a) said:

Injustice is of three types: First is the injustice that would not be forgiven, second is the injustice, which would not be left without appeal and the third is that which would be forgiven. The injustice which would not be forgiven is polytheism with the Almighty Allah. The Quran says:

"Surely Allah does not forgive that anything should be associated with Him..." (4:48)

As for the injustice that would be forgiven is a small injustice that everyone commits on himself, but the injustice that would not be left without accounting includes the injustice of people on one another; they would have to compensate for it very dearly. It is not like receiving an injury or being lashed, on the contrary it is most painful.[98]

The Messenger of Allah (s) said:

---

[98] Biharul Anwar, Vol. 7, Pg. 271

"One who fears retaliation should refrain from oppressing others."[99]

The accounting about the rights of people on Judgment Day is very difficult, because there one would have nothing which one could give to the claimants; for example one who usurped the property of others in the world, or did not bear the expenses of wife or children, or one who killed a person and did not pay the blood money, or striked an oppressed one and did not pay its penalty, or seriously harmed someone and did not recompense, or backbitten about someone or insulted another, but did not convince that person to forgive him, in Qiyamat and at the time of appeal, he has nothing which he can offer to those who have a claim on him.

This problem can be solved only in one of the two ways: the first is that the good deeds of the debtor can be swapped with those of the creditor to compensate for that which he had usurped in the world and the next option is that if the debtor does not have any good deeds in his account, an equal quantum of sins may be transferred from the account of the creditor to the scroll of deeds of the debtor as compensation.

A person has narrated from Imam Muhammad Baqir ('a) or Imam Ja'far Sadiq ('a) that he said:

"The debtor would be brought in Qiyamat in such a state that he would be extremely terrified; if he has good deeds in his account, they would be taken from him and given to the claimants and if he does not have any good deeds in his account, sins of the claimant are transferred to the account of the debtor."[100]

The Messenger of Allah (s) said:

"A person would be brought before the Almighty Allah on Judgment Day for accounting and the scroll of deeds would be handed to him. When he looks at it, he would not find his good deeds in it. He would

---

[99] Kafi, Vol. 2, Pg. 335

[100] Biharul Anwar, Vol. 7, Pg. 274

say: O Lord, this is not my scroll of deeds, since I cannot see my good deeds in it. He would be told: Your Lord neither makes a mistake nor does He forget anything. Your good deeds are transferred to persons whose backbiting you committed. After that another person would be presented for accounting and his scroll of deeds would be handed to him. When he looks at it, he would find it containing a large number of worship acts, which he had never performed. He would say: O Lord, this is not my scroll of deeds, since it records good deeds that I have never performed. He would be told: Since so-and-so backbited about you, in exchange We transferred his good deeds to your account."[101]

The Messenger of Allah (s) also said:

"On Judgment Day, a group would be brought having huge good deeds like mountains in their accounts; but the Almighty Allah would disperse them as particles of dust; and they would be taken to Hell."

Salman asked: "O Messenger of Allah (s), who would these people be?"

He replied:

"They were of those who prayed, fasted and remained awake all night in prayers, but when unlawful things were presented to them, they simply pounced on it."[102]

The Messenger of Allah (s) asked his companions:

"Do you know who is poor?"

They replied: "It is one among us who neither has any money nor any goods."

The Messenger of Allah said:

"The real poor one among my followers is one who would come on Judgment Day with prayers, fasts and Zakat, while there would be some who have defamed others, accused some of fornication, usurped

---

[101] Jamius Sadaat, Vol. 3, Pg. 306

[102] Mustadrakul Wasail, Vol. 13, Pg. 63

others' property, killed someone and thrashed some; thus the good deeds of that first man would be taken and transferred to these sinners; if the good deeds would be depleted, but some claimants would still be there, then the sins of the claimants would be transferred to him, and he would be thrown into Hell."[103]

Difference in accounting

The accounting of all the people on Judgment Day is not the same; for some it is extremely easy and for some it is extremely difficult. Three kinds of accounting are described in the Holy Quran: Severe accounting, evil accounting and an easy accounting. These differences are due to the kinds of deeds of different people. Infidels, oppressors and sinners would face an extremely severe accounting. They have more evil traits of character and possess more sins and at the time of accounting, each of their acts will be checked in detail; this is true especially for oppressors. Who would be answerable in detail about their oppressions and ordered to compensate to those whose rights they had violated. But as for righteous believers, whose scroll of deeds will be given in their right hands, their accounting would be easy, since they would not be having any sin in it; or if there, they would be minor, requiring no accounting; their accounting would be over very fast and they would be happily sent to the Paradise to dwell in the neighborhood of the Prophet and the Imams.

The best way to escape the difficulties of accounting is that a person should be requited of his deeds in this world itself and before his death.

The Messenger of Allah (s) said:

"Evaluate your deeds before you are subjected to the accounting of your deeds on the balance; weigh your deeds yourself and in this way prepare yourself for the major accounting."[104]

---

[103] Biharul Anwar, Vol. 69, Pg. 6

[104] Wasailush Shia, Vol. 16, Pg. 100

How nice it would be if one devotes an hour to evaluate ones deeds every day. That one goes into isolation and in detail and without any indulgence evaluates the deeds of the past twenty-four hours. If he has performed all his duties, he should thank Allah and resolve to do the same in future also; on the contrary in a better way. should And if he omitted an obligatory duty, since it can be amended, he repents and makes up for it; if he has committed a sin, he repents for it along with a firm intention never to repeat it again. If he owes something to another person, he pays it immediately and earns the approval of his debtor; and if it is not possible to repay him immediately, he vows that he would obtain his approval at the first opportunity. He seeks the forgiveness of the Almighty Allah. He should be earnest to amend his account as if it is the last hour of his life in the world and his death is going to occur the next moment. Such people would not need to account for their deeds on Judgment Day and they would enter Paradise without accounting or after an easy accounting.

Swiftness in accounting

Accounting of all the people would be at one and the same time and it would be done very swiftly. This point is explained clearly in the verse of Quran:

"They shall have (their) portion of what they have earned, and Allah is swift in reckoning." (2:202)

"..And whoever disbelieves in the communications of Allah then surely Allah is quick in reckoning." (3:19)

"...These it is that have their reward with their Lord; surely Allah is quick in reckoning."(3:199)

"...And be careful of (your duty to) Allah; surely Allah is swift in reckoning." (5:4)

"And Allah pronounces a doom- there is no repeller of His decree, and He is swift to take account." (13:41)

"That Allah may requite each soul (according to) what it has earned; surely Allah is swift in reckoning." (14:51)

"This day every soul shall be rewarded for what it has earned; no injustice (shall be done) this day; surely Allah is quick in reckoning." (40:17)

"Then are they sent back to Allah, their Master, the True one; now surely His is the judgment and He is swiftest in taking account." (6:62)

From such verses it can be concluded that the Almighty Allah would take a swift account of all the small and big deeds of people and decide their fate.

Allamah Tabatabai has mentioned a few points under the explanation of these verses and in justification of a swift reckoning of the Almighty Allah:

1. The Almighty Allah is cognizant of every small and big, good and evil deed of all, whenever they might have committed them.

2. The actual good and bad deeds of the people would be recorded and they will change into another form and it is these which would be their recompense.

3. In the world and after every good and bad deed, its recompense is given to the people and the account is clear to the Almighty Allah, but it would become clear to the people on Judgment Day.[105]

A man asked Amirul Momineen ('a): "How would the Almighty Allah take the account of the people while they would be so numerous?"

He replied: "He does so just as He conveys their sustenance to them."

He asked: "How would he take their accounts while they do not see Him?"

He replied: "He does so just as He conveys their sustenance to them, while they do not see Him."[106]

This tradition can be explained as follows: Sustenance consists of things, which a man needs to enable him to survive and remain in health and well being. For example different types of foods, water, clothes, light, elements, air, medicine and…the Almighty Allah bestows sustenance to man; it implies that in the system of creation, He bestowed favor to the needs of all the people, anticipated all the causes and factors of sustenance of man and created them and placed the instruments of using them in his being. Action and creation of Allah is instantaneous and is not gradual, but the earning of sustenance by human beings is gradual and temporal. It is not that in conveying the sustenance to every person a new favor and intention is needed.

Allah is the creator of time and space; since His holy being is not in need of time and space; his action also is not gradual and time-bound:

"..And the matter of the hour is but as the twinkling of an

---

[105] Al-Mizan, Vol. 15, Pg. 132 & Vol. 12, Pg. 91

[106] Biharul Anwar, Vol. 7, Pg. 271

eye or it is still nearer." **(16:77)**

Same is the case with the accounting of deeds. The Almighty Allah has direct knowledge of all the deeds of the people. Their accounts and consequences are clear to Him and there is no need for separate accounting, although their fruits would be declared on Judgment Day.

Intercession (Shafa'ah)

Intercession of people is an important Islamic concept, which would be there at the time of accounting and on Judgment Day. Its negation and proof and limits and conditions have always been topics of discussion in scholastic theology and interpretation of Quran. True cognition of the meaning of intercession is very important for one who believes in Allah and the Judgment Day and who considers following the laws of Shariat to be the means of success and salvation in the hereafter. We shall study this important aspect under the following headings:

Definition of intercession

The literal meaning of intercession is mediation or recommendation of forgiveness or kindness with regard to a person deserving of mercy from another powerful person. Intercession is found in all small and big human societies and is even customary between members of a family and it is considered a necessary factor of social life. Intercession in a place creates an implication that a person or a powerful group of people control administration of social matters, and frame rules and regulations for those subordinate to them and they also fix rewards for those who obey and punishments for disobedient. In such a society if all the people perform their duties they would be rewarded for it and there would be no need of intercession; but if some of them oppose it, the ruler or rulers have the right to punish the wrong doer as they had promised.

But sometimes higher exigencies dictate that some of their mistakes be overlooked. It is in these circumstances that the possibility of intercession arises or that the ruling person himself is included in the action and by observing some qualities or good deeds, which he knows are present in the person who is to be interceded for, points which deserve mercy; in that case he forgives his crime and orders his release. Or that a respectable and well wishing personality interferes and asks the ruler to forgive. Sometimes the same action is taken with regard to some persons, who have performed their duties nicely and are given more rewards than that which is fixed for such deeds so that they may be appreciated and encouraged. However in any case, some points must not be overlooked:

One: Acceptance or rejection of intercession is under the discretion of ruler and criminals should not sin in hope that they would get intercession. Two: Intercession would not be without criteria; on the contrary it would be possible in circumstances that the person to be interceded should possess qualities making him eligible to be interceded for. The interceder does not ask the ruler to forsake the commands of his guardians or to disable the law of punishing criminals; on the contrary he mentions some specialties of the person to be interceded for and appeals to the greatness and mercy of the ruling person and keeping in mind the present exigencies, requests the ruler that he should exercise the rights of his rulership and have mercy on the person who is to be interceded for and that he should bestow his favor and forgiveness on him. Therefore, intercession is a social exigency and does not conflict with laws of recompense.

Intercession in Quran

Now it must be seen what Quran says about intercession. In this matter it is better to study the verses related to intercession:

Verses on this topic can be divided into different types:

First Group: Verses that apparently negate intercession

> "And be on your guard against a day when one soul shall not avail another in the least, neither shall intercession on its behalf be accepted, nor shall any compensation be taken from it, nor shall they be helped." (2:48)

> "And be on your guard against a day when no soul shall avail another in the least neither shall any compensation be accepted from it, nor shall intercession profit it, nor shall they be helped." (2:123)

> "O you who believe! spend out of what We have given you before the day comes in which there is no bargaining, neither any friendship nor intercession, and the unbelievers- they are the unjust." (2:254)

> "The day on which a friend shall not avail (his) friend aught, nor shall they be helped."(44:41)

Second Group: Negation of intercession for a Special Category

"...The unjust shall not have any compassionate friend nor any intercessor who should be obeyed." (40:18)

"And none but the guilty led us astray. So we have no intercessors, nor a true friend."(26:99-101)

"And warn with it those who fear that they shall be gathered to their Lord- there is no guardian for them, nor any intercessor besides Him- that they may guard (against evil)."(6:51)

Third Group: Verses that limit intercession to Allah

"Say: Allah's is the intercession altogether; His is the kingdom of the heavens and the earth, then to Him you shall be brought back." (39:44)

"Surely the day of separation is their appointed term, of all of them. The day on which a friend shall not avail (his) friend aught, nor shall they be helped. Save those on whom Allah shall have mercy; surely He is the Mighty the Merciful." (44:40-42)

Fourth Group: Proof of intercession by the approval of Allah

"On that day shall no intercession avail except of him whom the Beneficent God allows and whose word He is pleased with." *(20:109)*

"..And they do not intercede except for him whom He approves, and for fear of Him they tremble." *(21:28)*

"And intercession will not avail aught with Him save of him whom He permits." *(34:23)*

"And how many an angel is there in the heavens whose intercession does not avail at all except after Allah has given permission to whom He pleases and chooses." *(53:26)*

"Surely your Lord is Allah, Who created the heavens and the earth in six periods, and He is firm in power, regulating the affair, there is no intercessor except after His permission."*(10:3)*

Reconciling the different types of verses

To reconcile different types of verses, it can be said that:

Firstly: Intercession is the right of the Almighty Allah and it is limited only to Him and in this aspect has no fixed limit, since He is the true owner of all existing things. All are in need of Him and He alone is absolutely needless. All causes and effects since in their own being, are in need of the creator of the world, in their causation and action also are attached to Him, so that whenever He desires He may take their being, causation and effect. And in this regard, additions and negation of additions to His qualities like: beneficence, generosity, forgiveness, kindness, force and anger are mediums and intercession is also in the same meaning. What was mentioned was with regard to innate matters; it is the same in legislative matters also. Reward and punishment of people on Judgment Day is also at discretion of Almighty Allah and no one can interfere in it, except through His permission and approval. Therefore intercession is also under His discretion.

Secondly: Other than the Almighty Allah other people may also intercede, but subject to the fact that Almighty Allah should accord them permission to intercede and that He should accept their intercession.

Thirdly: Those who would be permitted to intercede are only those who can intercede; as Almighty Allah has approved their intercession. Therefore intercession is not without criterion and it originates from particular circumstances of one who is to be interceded for.

Who all would be included in intercession?

Now let us see who would be included in intercession of the intercessors.

In this matter also, the best solution is to refer to verses of Quran:

The Holy Quran says:

"The day on which We will gather those who guard (against evil) to the Beneficent God to receive honors. And We will drive the guilty to hell, thirsty. They shall not control intercession, save he who has made a covenant with the Beneficent God." (19:85-87)

It can be concluded from this verse that only those would be able to benefit from intercession that are promised intercession from Almighty Allah. In the interpretation of this promise it can be said: The Almighty Allah, glorified be He, in the Holy Quran has limited His forgiveness only to those who give up particular sins or subjected it to performance of particular good deeds. For example it says: If you refrain from so-and-so, I will forgive your other bad deeds also. And this in itself is a sort of promise between Allah and His servants, and the Almighty Allah would invariably fulfill His promise. This is the meaning of intercession of Allah and intercessors with Allah. One of those promises is glad tiding of acceptance of repentance of sinners as clearly mentioned in verses of Quran.

The Holy Quran says:

"And (as to) those who do evil deeds, then repent after that and believe, your Lord after that is most surely Forgiving, Merciful." (7:153)

And also says:

"And He it is Who accepts repentance from His servants and pardons the evil deeds and He knows what you do." (42:25)

Further it says:

"Except him who repents and believes and does a good deed; so these are they of whom Allah changes the evil deeds to good ones; and Allah is Forgiving, Merciful." (25:70)

Another group, which is promised forgiveness by the Almighty Allah, is of those who have faith in Allah, the Prophet and resurrection and those who are pious and who refrain from greater sins.

The Holy Quran says:

> *"If you shun the great sins which you are forbidden, We will do away with your small sins and cause you to enter an honorable place of entering." (4:31)*

And also says:

> *"That is the command of Allah which He has revealed to you, and whoever is careful of (his duty to) Allah, He will remove from him his evil and give him a big reward."(65:5)*

It also says:

> *"O you who believe! be careful of (your duty to) Allah and believe in His Apostle: He will give you two portions of His mercy, and make for you a light with which you will walk, and forgive you, and Allah is Forgiving, Merciful." (57:28)*

Quran has also said:

> *"He will put your deeds into a right state for you, and forgive you your faults; and whoever obeys Allah and His Apostle, he indeed achieves a mighty success." (33:71)*

Whatever was mentioned was about the promise of the Almighty Allah that He would overlook some sins subject to particular conditions.

The glorified Lord has also promised the righteous an increase in rewards. The Quran says:

"Whoever brings a good deed, he shall have ten like it, and whoever brings an evil deed, he shall be recompensed only with the like of it, and they shall not be dealt with unjustly."(6:160)

Ibne Abi Umair says: I heard Imam Musa Kazim ('a) say:

Every believer who keeps away from greater sins, would not be interrogated about his small sins. The Almighty Allah says:

"If you shun the great sins which you are forbidden, We will do away with your small sins and cause you to enter an honorable place of entering. (4:31)"

Then the reporter asked: "In whose favor would intercession take place?"

The Imam replied:

"My father has narrated from his father from Imam Ali ('a) and he has narrated from the Messenger of Allah (s) that he said: My intercession is for those who have committed greater sins; as for the righteous, they would have no problem."

Ibne Abi Umair asked: "O son of Allah's Messenger, how would intercession be done for sinners of great sins when the Almighty Allah has said:

"…And they do not intercede except for him whom He approves… (21:28)

That is I will never forgive one who has committed great sins?"

Imam ('a) said:

"The real believer, whenever he commits a sin, he becomes restless and regretful and the Holy Prophet (s) has said: Regret is enough for repentance and he said: One who is pleased on performing a good deed and is regretful on committing a sin is a believer...and one who is not regretful of his sins is not a believer and intercession would not benefit him."[107]

If faith is taken in this meaning, it can be said: Most or all the believers would enter Paradise by intercession of the Holy Prophet (s).

Quran says:

"And soon will your Lord give you so that you shall be well pleased." (93:5)

The Messenger of Allah (s) said:

"The Almighty Allah has left a matter at my discretion, and I delayed it till Judgment Day so that I may intercede for the believers."[108]

In the same way, the Holy Prophet (s) said:

"When I assume the seat at the Praised Station (Maqaam Mahmood), I would intercede for those sinners of my nation who have committed greater sins and it would be accepted by the Almighty Allah. But by Allah, I would not intercede for anyone who had harassed my descendants."[109]

With reference to these verses and traditions and tens of similar statements, intercession cannot be rejected as a whole. The Almighty Allah has promised it to sinners and He would definitely keep His word. But the promise of intercession is not such that should abrogate the foundations of Shariat laws and religious duties as a result of which in

---

[107] Wasailush Shia, Vol. 15, Pg. 335

[108] Biharul Anwar, Vol. 8, Pg. 37

[109] Biharul Anwar, Vol. 8, Pg. 37

hope of intercession, people commit all sorts of sins. Laws and rules of Shariat, obligatory duties and prohibited acts have grown through actual exigencies and evils; the straight path is specified only for perfection of humanity and wayfaring to Allah, which may guarantee spiritual salvation and save from destructions. Paradise and bounties of Paradise; Hell and chastisements of Hell are there as a result of good and bad deeds in the world. Therefore anyone who commits a bad deed would definitely be recompensed for it in the world or the hereafter, except that he should repent before death and make amends for his behavior.

The following points must also not be overlooked:

Firstly: Even if you suppose that some sinners would be included in intercession, you should know that intercession is only in Qiyamat; and as mentioned in traditions, Barzakh is not the place for intercession.

Amr bin Yazid says: I asked Imam Ja'far Sadiq ('a): "I have heard that you said:

All our Shias would go to Paradise?"

He replied:

"Yes, I said it and I am right; by Allah, all of them would enter Paradise."

The narrator asked: "May I be your ransom, even if they have numerous great sins to their credit?"

The Imam said:

"As for Judgment Day, all of you would enter Paradise through intercession of the Prophet or his successor. But I am fearful about you with regard to Barzakh."

The narrator asked: "What is Barzakh?"

He replied:

It is there from the time of death and burial upto Judgment Day."[110]

---

[110] Biharul Anwar, Vol. 6, Pg. 267

Chastisements of Barzakh and the long period of it should not considered minor according to traditional reports, it is a sample of the chastisement of Hell.

Secondly: Hardships and back breaking difficulties of Judgment Day; and the accounting of deeds of the sinners also must not be overlooked.

Thirdly: It is correct that a large number of believer sinners would be saved from entering Hell through the intercession of Prophet and other intercessors, but all would not be like this; on the contrary those who committed more and deadlier sins, would be sent to Hell to wash off their crimes and after a period of time, less or more, after tasting chastisement, in the end would be saved from punishment of Hell through the intercession of intercessors and finally enter Paradise; hence the true believer in monotheism would never remain in Hell forever.

Fourthly: That which is promised is intercession with regard to believers and monotheists and committing some great sins especially committing them repeatedly may lead to loss of faith; in that case one would not be included in intercession.

Fifthly: Although the glorified Lord has promised intercession to the doers of greater sins, it would never be unconditional. It is not known who would be included in it, with what conditions and in what position they would be.

From all that was mentioned so far we can conclude that committing sin in hope of intercession is the greatest fallacy.

Who would intercede?

In the above-mentioned verses, intercession is proved for the Almighty Allah, absolutely, without any limit and for angels, through the approval of Allah, although their intercession is innate. In the same way it is proved for the Holy Prophet of Islam (s), under the permission of Allah:

"And soon will your Lord give you so that you shall be well

pleased." (93:5)

Although after reconciling the unequivocal traditions recorded about this. Except for these circumstances, Quran does not declare intercession for anyone else, but it has also not denied it, if it is by the permission of Allah.

However in traditions, intercession is proved for other groups also:

a) Quran and memorizers of Quran; and those who act on it.

b) Successors of the Prophet and the Infallible Imams ('a).

c) Lady Fatima ('a), the respected daughter of the Prophet and the mother of the Holy Imams ('a).

d) Martyrs who laid down their lives in defense of Islam.

e) Divine scholars who propagated Islam verbally, practically and through their writings and who have a role in guidance of people.

Lastly, we think that it is necessary to mention a few points:

1. Power of intercession would depend on the role of intercessors in spread of Islam and how faithful they were to its rules and regulations.

2. Intercessors would intercede for their own followers and not for everyone else.

3. Their intercession would depend on permission of Almighty Allah.

4. Intercession will not be like a business deal without criteria and based on whims without any eligibility in one who is interceded for.

Therefore, it is but a great fallacy and a satanic deception to avoid religious duties and to consider sins as minor hoping in intercession of intercessors.

Siraat Bridge

Siraat is in the meaning of a 'path'. The pathway between two houses is called as Siraat, which is mostly marked with a sign. But the words of 'Siraat' and 'path' are also sometimes used for things other than pathways related to space or place. It is often said: Path of life, path of prosperity, path of progress…and this term is also used in the sense of the medium of reaching ones destination.

In this world, willingly or unwillingly, man is headed to death and the world of the hereafter.

The Holy Quran says:

> "O man! surely you must strive (to attain) to your Lord, a hard striving until you meet Him." (84:6)

The distance between birth to death and all beliefs, views, morals, speech, character and behavior of man, during this period is a real route, but it is not confined to space; and willingly or unwillingly, one has to traverse it. It can be called as the path or way of life.

In order to traverse this path, man walks on a straight line which is the shortest, smoothest and easiest and free of danger way and in the Holy Quran it is called the straight path (Siraat Mustaqeem). Or he deviates from the straight path, going into valleys of misguidance and continues to wander aimlessly. The Holy Quran has introduced worship of only one God and submission to His commands, according to pure nature of man and to which the divine prophets have called people as the straight path (Siraat Mustaqeem).

> *"Surely Allah is my Lord and your Lord, therefore serve Him; this is the right path." (3:51)*

> *"And this is the path of your Lord, (a) right (path); indeed We have made the communications clear for a people who mind." (6:126)*

> *"Say: Surely, (as for) me, my Lord has guided me to the right path; (to) a most right religion, the faith of Ibrahim the upright one, and he was not of the polytheists. Say: Surely my prayer and my sacrifice and my life and my death are (all) for Allah, the Lord of the worlds" (6:161-2)*

> *"Did I not charge you, O children of Adam! that you should not serve the Shaitan? Surely he is your open enemy. And that you should serve Me; this is the right way." (36:60-61)*

Therefore, the straight path (Siraat Mustaqeem) can be interpreted as referring to Almighty Allah and entry into Paradise from: the right beliefs, good morals, laws and rules of Shariat sent through divine prophets. The straight path (Siraat Mustaqeem) is one, not more and every other way other than it is deviated. The Holy Quran says in the following verses:

> "And most surely those who do not believe in the hereafter are deviating from the way."(23:74)

> "...And whoever adopts unbelief instead of faith, he indeed has lost the right direction of the way." (2:108)

> "...(As for) those who go astray from the path of Allah, they shall surely have a severe punishment because they forgot the day of reckoning." (38:26)

> "Gather together those who were unjust and their associates, and what they used to worship Besides Allah, then lead them to the way to hell." (37:22-23)

Therefore the Siraat is the way of life, which begins in this world and continues till Judgment Day. This way can be divided into two: straight path and wayward path. The straight path is a collection of right beliefs, good morals, laws and rules of Shariat and wayward paths consist of invalid beliefs, bad morals and unethical speech and action, which are against Shariat.

The seeker of this way is a man who through his free will, chooses one of these two paths and walks on them.

These paths are real and not notional. Every person by choosing the type of faith, morals and intentions in his inner being or in path of humanity performs servitude to gain divine proximity, perfection and illumination. Or he proceeds on path of bestiality and darkness and seeks distance from Allah to fall into terrifying valleys of materialism. Every person in this world treads on one of these paths, even though he might be unaware of it. The same path continues after death in the world of Barzakh and Qiyamat and it end either at Paradise or Hell; in other words it can be said: Siraat in Qiyamat is the unseen version of this same worldly Siraat, which would become clear there. The same meaning is indicated in traditions.

Mufaddal bin Umar says: I asked Imam Ja'far Sadiq ('a): "What is Siraat?"

He replied:

"It is the path of divine recognition and knowing Allah, the Mighty and Sublime. Siraat is of two types: Siraat in the world and Siraat in hereafter. As for Siraat in the world it denotes obedience of the Imam whose obedience is necessary; whoever recognizes him in the world and follows his commands, would be able to cross the Siraat in hereafter which is like a bridge over Hell. And one who does not recognize him in the world (and does not benefit from his guidance) he would stumble in the hereafter and fall into Hell."[111]

It is narrated from Imam Hasan Askari ('a) that he said:

"True paths are two: One is in this world and another in the Hereafter. The Siraat Mustaqeem in this world is one, which does not contain excessiveness, defects and shortcomings. It is the straight road, which never drifts to untruth. Siraat of Hereafter is one, which leads the faithful believer straight to Paradise. Those following this path, will never turn from Paradise towards Hell, but will reach it straight

---

[111] Biharul Anwar, Vol. 8, Pg. 66

away."[112]

Abu Huraira has narrated from the Holy Prophet (s) that he said:

Jibraeel (Archangel Gabriel) came down to me and said: "Shall I not give you glad tidings of Paradise, through which you may cross the path (Siraat)?" I asked: "Why not!" He said: "You will cross it by effulgence (Noor) of Allah; and Ali by your effulgence (Noor), which is effulgence (Noor) of Allah. And your community will cross it through effulgence (Noor) of Ali, which is your effulgence (Noor); and one who is not given a light by the Almighty Allah would have no light."[113]

Shaykh Mufeed says:

Siraat literary means a pathway and that is why religion is called Siraat, since it is the way of gaining divine rewards and for the same reason guardianship (Wilayat) and following Imam Ali ('a) and the Holy Imams ('a) is called Siraat. Therefore Amirul Momineen ('a) said: I am the straight path (Siraat Mustaqeem) of Allah and a stable handle which will not break." He means to say that his recognition and attachment to him is the path to Almighty Allah.[114]

Abu Basir has narrated from Imam Ja'far Sadiq ('a) that he said:

"Different types of people would cross the Siraat Bridge. Siraat is finer than hair and sharper than sword. Some would pass over it like a flash of lightning and some would gallop over it like a horse, some would crawl over it on their four limbs and chests; some would traverse it on foot; some would be hanging from it; sometimes the fire of Hell would apprehend them and sometimes it would leave them."[115]

Therefore the crossing of Siraat Bridge is not same for all. On the contrary it depends on their cognition of religion and Shariat and is

---

[112] Tafsir Imam Hasan Askari (a.s.), Pg. 44

[113] Biharul Anwar, Vol. 8, Pg. 69

[114] Biharul Anwar, Vol. 8, Pg. 70

[115] Biharul Anwar, Vol. 8, Pg. 64

subject to their familiarity with the law of Shariah and avoidance of disobedience and sins.

The accurate recognition of the straight path; honesty, sincerity for it and being bound to it and absence of deviation from it is a difficult job. That is why it requires divine help; and that is why Muslims in all obligatory and recommended prayers always beseech Almighty Allah to keep them on the straight path:

"Keep us on the right path." (1:6)

Imam Khomeini says with regard to Siraat:

Presently we are in the Siraat Mustaqeem; it is the same path on one end of which is the world and on the other is the hereafter and we are walking on this Siraat Mustaqeem. The curtain, which is raised at that time, is the path of Hell (Siraat Jahannam), which passes through Hell; that is it engulfs the fire of Hell; it passes through the middle of this place. You have to cross it from here. World is this same kind. Corruption is that same fire, which has surrounded you, you have to cross this same corruption in such a way that you cross it safely.[116]

And he says:

All of us are on the straight path and it crosses over Hell, its reality would be exposed in that world. In this matter every person has a particular path with him, and is on a journey (wayfaring) or is on the straight path, which ends at Paradise or higher; or the deviated path to the left or deviated to the right; both would end at Hell.[117]

He also says:

The path which is stretched to Hell; if you walk straight in this world, you would be rejected from that path straight away, the inward Hell of

---

[116] Maad az Deedgah Imam Khomeini, Pg. 278

[117] Maad az Deedgah Imam Khomeini, Pg. 278

this world; if you walk straight from this path and do not deviate to the left or the right, you would cross the Siraat Bridge of this world also directly; but you should neither turn left nor right; if you turn to the left there is Hell and if you turn to the right it is Hell.[118]

---

[118] Maad az Deedgah Imam Khomeini, Pg. 281

Hell

Hell is a place in another world where the sinners would be punished with various kinds of chastisements. The Holy Quran has mentioned is as 'jahannam' and 'jaheem'. Please pay attention to the following verses:

"Say to those who disbelieve: You shall be vanquished, and driven together to hell; and evil is the resting-place." (3:12)

"...Surely Allah will gather together the hypocrites and the unbelievers all in hell." (4:140)

"Allah has promised the hypocritical men and the hypocritical women and the unbelievers the fire of hell to abide therein; it is enough for them; and Allah has cursed them and they shall have lasting punishment." (9:68)

"Whoever comes to his Lord (being) guilty, for him is surely hell; he shall not die therein, nor shall he live." (20:74)

"And (as for) those who disbelieve, for them is the fire of hell; it shall not be finished with them entirely so that they should die, nor shall the chastisement thereof be lightened to them: even thus do We retribute every ungrateful one." (35:36)

"And your Lord says: Call upon Me, I will answer you; surely those who are too proud for My service shall soon enter hell abased." (40:60)

Punishments of Hell

Quran has described the punishments of Hell to be severe and painful and has mentioned them in the following terms:

'Painful chastisement', 'degrading chastisement', 'great chastisement', 'severe chastisement', 'evil resort' and 'burning chastisement'.

The most important chastisement of Hell is the chastisement of fire; that is why Hell is also mentioned in numerous verses of Quran as Fire; for example:

"And (as to) those who disbelieve in and reject My communications, they are the inmates of the fire, in it they shall abide." (2:39)
"Yea! whoever earns evil and his sins beset him on every side, these are the inmates of the fire; in it they shall abide." (2:81)

All the chastisements of Hell are mentioned as various kinds of blazing and scorching fires.

Food of the folks of Hell

The Holy Quran says:

> "Surely We have prepared for the iniquitous a fire, the curtains of which shall encompass them about; and if they cry for water, they shall be given water like molten brass which will scald their faces; evil the drink..." (18:29)

> "Hell is before him and he shall be given to drink of festering water: He will drink it little by little and will not be able to swallow it agreeably, and death will come to him from every quarter, but he shall not die; and there shall be vehement chastisement before him."(14:16-17)

> "Surely the tree of the Zaqqum is the food of the sinful, like dregs of oil; it shall boil in (their) bellies, like the boiling of hot water." (44:43-46)

Dress of the folks of Hell

The Almighty Allah says in the Holy Quran:

> "As to those who disbelieve, for them are cut out garments of fire, boiling water shall be poured over their heads with it shall be melted what is in their bellies and (their) skins as well. And for them are whips of iron." (22:19-21)

As you can see, Hell is mentioned in the Holy Quran as a place full of blazing and scorching fire and which greets its inmates with dresses and foods of fire. Is the condition really as concluded from the apparent meaning of the verses? Is the fire of Hell same as the fires of this world or of some other kind that its like is not found in the world? In some verses are mentioned qualities of the fire of Hell, whose like is not present in the world.

And He says:

> "...Then be on your guard against the fire of which men and stones are the fuel; it is prepared for the unbelievers." *(Surah Baqarah 2:24)*

And He also says:

> "O you who believe! save yourselves and your families from a fire whose fuel is men and stones..." *(66:6)*

And He further says:

> "Surely you and what you worship besides Allah are the firewood of hell; to it you shall come." *(21:98)*

In these verses, the souls of men and their deities, whether it be idols or precious stones are described as fuel and flames of blazing fire of Hell and such a thing is not present in the fire of the world.

In the Holy Quran, the Almighty Allah says:

> "(As for) those who swallow the property of the orphans unjustly, surely they only swallow fire into their bellies and they shall enter burning fire." *(4:10)*

And He says:

> *"..And (as for) those who hoard up gold and silver and do not spend it in Allah's way, announce to them a painful chastisement. On the day when it shall be heated in the fire of hell, then their foreheads and their sides and their backs shall be branded with it; this is what you hoarded up for yourselves, therefore taste what you hoarded." (9:34-35)*

In the above mentioned verses, swallowing the property of orphan is directly mentioned as swallowing flames of fire and hoarding of gold and silver is mentioned as means of punishment. The hoarder would exclaim: "These were what I had hoarded," and he would taste it.

The Holy Quran says with regard to punishment of the folks of Hell:

> *"(As for) those who disbelieve in Our communications, We shall make them enter fire; so oft as their skins are thoroughly burned, We will change them for other skins, that they may taste the chastisement; surely Allah is Mighty, Wise." (4:56)*

It is concluded from this verse that fire of Hell is neither like the fire of the world nor the body of man, which would be punished would be like the body in the world. Fires of the world scorch the body of man and not his soul and mind; but Holy Quran says: Fire of Hell would reach upto the soul of man and scorch his conscience. Quran says:

> *"It is the fire kindled by Allah, which rises above the hearts. Surely it shall be closed over upon them in extended columns." (104:6-9)*

From such verses, it can be concluded that fire of Hell is basically different from fire of the world and it is having completely different qualities. Basically if the fire of Hell had been like the fire of the world, it would have been the world and not the hereafter.

Statements of Imam Khomeini

Here we shall mention some statements of Imam Khomeini which describe Hell and the inmates of Hell:

Hell, various chastisements of the ethereal world and Qiyamat are forms of your own deeds and morals. You have with your own hands put yourself into degradation and trouble and still continue to do that; you walk to Hell with your own feet and prepare Hell with your own deeds. Hell is nothing but the essence of your evil deeds; darkness and loneliness of the grave and purgatory is not but the shadow of oppressive invalid morals of man:

"So he who has done an atom's weight of good shall see it. And he who has done an atom's weight of evil shall see it." **(99:7-8)**[119]

And he says:

Here you usurped the property of an orphan and enjoyed it. The Almighty Allah knows the form of it that you will see in Hell, and what is that degradation that is in your destiny? Here you bad mouthed people; harassed and tortured them; Allah knows what the punishment of this mental torture of people is. In that world, when you see you would understand what chastisements you have prepared for yourself. When you backbited, its ethereal form was prepared for you. It would be rejected with you. You would be raised with it and you will taste its

---

[119] Maad az Deedgah Imam Khomeini, Pg. 301

chastisement.[120]

And he also says:

The Almighty Allah informs in the Book revealed by Him in the holy verse:

"It is the fire kindled by Allah, which rises above the hearts." (104:6-9)

...About the quality of fire – which is the fire of Allah – it will inundate the hearts and scorch them; no fire scorches the hearts, except the fire of Allah. All the fire of Hell and chastisement of grave and Qiyamat and others which you mistakenly compared to be the fire of the world and the chastisement of the world; you made a wrong conclusion and the fire in this world is supposedly cool matter, the punishment of this world is very easy, your understanding is defective and short in this world; even if all the fires of the world collective try, they cannot burn the soul of man, there is another fire, which can scorch the body, scorch the soul and melts and scorch the hearts.[121]

Threatened with chastisement of Hell

In Quran some people are threatened with chastisement of Hell:

First group, Infidels: those who did not have faith in Allah, resurrection and prophethood. Quran says:

"And (as to) those who disbelieve in and reject My communications, they are the inmates of the fire, in it they shall abide." (2:39)

---

[120] Maad az Deedgah Imam Khomeini, Pg. 305

[121] Maad az Deedgah Imam Khomeini, Pg. 315

Second group, Polytheists: Those who associated someone or something in the worship of Almighty Allah. The Holy Quran says:

> *"Surely those who disbelieve from among the followers of the Book and the polytheists shall be in the fire of hell, abiding therein; they are the worst of men." (98:6)*

Third group, Hypocrites: Those who had no sincerity in faith; they only made a verbal claim and lived among believers. With regard to them the Quran says:

> *"Allah has promised the hypocritical men and the hypocritical women and the unbelievers the fire of hell to abide therein; it is enough for them; and Allah has cursed them and they shall have lasting punishment." (9:68)*

In these verses, these three groups are promised Hell and it is also declared that their stay in Hell would be forever. The terms of perpetuity are especially used in this regard. But we should know that perpetuity only applies to something that would continue forever and there is no other meaning of this term.

Raghib writes: "Perpetual' is something that is going to endure for a long time and that why when a person has grey hair it is said that he is a perpetual man. After that the term is used figuratively for someone who is going to live forever.[122]

Ibne Athir has also commented on the tradition of Imam Ali ('a) in which he said: 'One who relies on the world and becomes inseparable

---

[122] Al-Mufradat, Pg. 154, under the word of 'KH-L-D'

from it', and explained the word of living forever in the sense of perpetuity.[123]

Therefore there is no doubt that infidels, polytheists and hypocrites would be chastised in Hell for a long time, since the Holy Quran has explained it in this way; although their remaining thus forever is a matter of doubt, especially with reference to two important points: one is that punishment of Hell is not a reprisal of enmity and taking revenge, on the contrary it is aimed to clean darkness and satanic filth and to gain eligibility of divine grace. The second point is that we must not forget the vastness of divine mercy and the fact that it precedes divine anger. Therefore, if due to the effect of prolonged punishment of folks of Hell on their monotheistic nature, which was concealed in their beings, is exposed, and the aspect of their humanity overcomes the animal and satanic aspect, it is possible that he would be included in grace and mercy of Allah who is the most merciful of all mercifuls and did not cease to exist. But we, along with our defective intellect and narrow mindedness do not have the right to adjudicate this important matter.

Fourth group, Oppressors: The Quran says:

> *"Then it shall be said to those who were unjust: Taste abiding chastisement; you are not requited except for what you earned." (10:52)*

Fifth group, those who have killed a human being without any justification: The Holy Quran says:

---

[123] Al-Nihaya, Vol. 2, Pg. 61, under the word of 'KH-L-D'

"And whoever kills a believer intentionally, his punishment is hell; he shall abide in it, and Allah will send His wrath on him and curse him and prepare for him a painful chastisement." (4:93)

There is no doubt that these groups, since they have committed very serious sins, should be punished for a long time in Hell due to their evil deeds; but as for their remaining in Hell forever, there is doubt about it as concluded from the apparent meaning of the verses; especially keeping in mind the two points mentioned before.

Sixth group, sinners and criminals: In the Holy Quran, the Almighty Allah says:

"Yea! Whoever earns evil and his sins beset him on every side, these are the inmates of the fire; in it they shall abide." (2:81)

And He also says:

"Surely the guilty shall abide in the chastisement of hell." (43:74)

As you can see, criminals and sinners are threatened that they would be thrown into Hell and into an everlasting chastisement. But with reference to a large number of verses and traditions, entry into Hell is conditional to firstly that he has died without repenting for his sins and secondly their chastisement of Hell and hardships of Qiyamat were not to the limit to enable them to become eligible for intercession, otherwise they would not have been in Hell. In these verses, it is mentioned that those who have been put into Hell and who were also threatened with everlasting punishment, but with regard to the points we mentioned before, their stay in Hell would be only according to the seriousness of their sins, and after being purified and becoming eligible for intercession through intercessors and unlimited grace and mercy of Almighty Allah would be freed from chastisement of Hell.

Seventh group, unaware infidels: Some had no faith in Allah, the Prophet and resurrection; but it was not due to innate hostility, on the contrary it was due to ignorance and unawareness. Like wild animals or half wild animals in wilderness or isolation; who lived like beasts and didn't know anything except eating, drinking and satisfying lust. Or that they had faith in their ancestral faith, without giving a thought to investigate it. Although such people are not eligible for Paradise, they would also not be punished in Hell, since the punishment of such unaware persons is not compatible with justice of Allah. The Almighty Allah says in the Holy Quran:

"Nor do We chastise until We raise an apostle." (17:15)

Paradise and its bounties

Paradise means a better world, a place with a pleasing atmosphere and full of varying bounties, in which the righteous would live after death. The Holy Quran has mentioned it as 'Garden', which denotes a place full of greenery and trees. In Quran, there are numerous verses, which promise Paradise to the believers and enumerate its different beauties and bounties; some of which are as follows:

> "And convey good news to those who believe and do good deeds, that they shall have gardens in which rivers flow; whenever they shall be given a portion of the fruit thereof, they shall say: This is what was given to us before; and they shall be given the like of it, and they shall have pure mates in them, and in them, they shall abide." (2:25)

> "But as to those who are careful of (their duty to) their Lord, they shall have gardens beneath which rivers flow, abiding in them; an entertainment from their Lord, and that which

is with Allah is best for the righteous." (3:198)

"Allah has promised to the believing men and the believing women gardens, beneath which rivers flow, to abide in them, and goodly dwellings in gardens of perpetual abode; and best of all is Allah's goodly pleasure- that is the grand achievement." (9:72)

"A likeness of the garden which the righteous are promised; there now beneath it rivers, its food and shades are perpetual; this is the requital of those who guarded (against evil), and the requital of the unbelievers is the fire." (13:35)

"The gardens of perpetuity, they shall enter them, rivers flowing beneath them; they shall have in them what they please. Thus does Allah reward those who guard (against evil)."(16:31)

"Surely (as for) those who believe and do good, We do not waste the reward of him who does a good work. These it is for whom are gardens of perpetuity beneath which rivers flow, ornaments shall be given to them therein of bracelets of gold, and they shall wear green robes of fine silk and thick silk brocade interwoven with gold, reclining therein on raised couches; excellent the recompense and goodly the resting place." (18:30-31)

"So no soul knows what is hidden for them of that which will refresh the eyes; a reward for what they did." (32:17)

"Those who believed in Our communications and were submissive: Enter the garden, you and your wives; you shall be made happy. There shall be sent round to them golden bowls and drinking-cups and therein shall be what their souls yearn after and (wherein) the eyes shall delight, and you shall abide therein. And this is the garden which you are given as an inheritance on account of what you did. For you therein are many fruits of which you shall eat." (43:69-73)

"A parable of the garden which those guarding (against evil) are promised: Therein are rivers of water that does not alter, and rivers of milk the taste whereof does not change, and rivers of drink delicious to those who drink, and rivers of honey clarified and for them therein are all fruits and protection from their Lord. (Are these) like those who abide in the fire..." (47:15)

"Hasten to forgiveness from your Lord and to a garden the extensiveness of which is as the extensiveness of the heaven and the earth; it is prepared for those who believe in Allah and His apostles..." (57:21)

"Surely the righteous shall drink of a cup the admixture of which is camphor A fountain from which the servants of Allah shall drink; they make it to flow a (goodly) flowing forth." (76:5-6)

"And reward them, because they were patient, with garden and silk. Reclining therein on raised couches, they shall find therein neither (the severe heat of) the sun nor intense cold. And close down upon them (shall be) its shadows, and its fruits shall be made near (to them), being easy to reach. And *there shall be made to go round about them vessels of silver and goblets which are of glass. (Transparent as) glass, made of silver; they have measured them according to a measure. And they shall be made to drink therein a cup the admixture of which shall be ginger. (Of) a fountain therein which is named Salsabil. And round about them shall go youths never altering in age; when you see them you will think them to be scattered pearls. And when you see there, you shall see blessings and a great kingdom. Upon them shall be garments of fine green silk and thick silk interwoven with gold, and they shall be adorned with bracelets of silver, and their Lord shall make them drink a pure drink." (76:12-21)*

The above verses describe Paradise as a place of extremely high standards and pleasing atmosphere in which different types of bounties are ready. They include verdant trees below which streams of sweet water flow; different delicious and fragrance fruits, which would be obtained without any efforts; brooks of clean milk and honey and pure wine flow there; whenever they want they can drink from it; fowl meat is ready for them; they recline on comfortable sofas in beautiful palaces and handsome servants continuously go around them entertaining them. They wear dresses of fine and soft garments and stroll in the gardens of Paradise; there would be Houries of Paradise for them, who are extremely beautiful and no man has touched them before this and they have not even looked at any man, except their consorts; and the righteous believers would have to just mention whatever he wants and it would be made available to him in Paradise.

It is mentioned that the above mentioned bounties are similar to the bounties of the world and it is necessary to accept this fact, but it is not necessary that we should consider them exactly as worldly examples having all worldly aspects and defects; if it had been so, Paradise would have been a part of the world, and not of hereafter. In the circumstance that hereafter is a very lofty, world which is not in the whole world; matters of the hereafter are pure of the defects of the matters of the world.

In some verses and traditions also the same excellence is mentioned and below we present some of them by way of examples:

The foods in the world are tasty, but along with it they have additional matters which must necessarily be expelled in urine and feces; but the foods of Paradise do not create excrement. Fruits of the world have to be picked, but the branches of fruits of Paradise would themselves come to the believer:

> *"And close down upon them (shall be) its shadows, and its fruits shall be made near (to them), being easy to reach." (76:14)*

Waters and milk of the world are prone to go bad if they are left for a long time, and their taste undergoes a change, but the water and milk of Paradise do not go bad:

> *"Therein are rivers of water that does not alter, and rivers of milk the taste whereof does not change." (47:15)*

Worldly drinks are tasty, but they also lead to intoxication and addiction; as opposed to drinks of Paradise, which are tasty but are pure of the defects of the worldly drinks.

Whatever is mentioned especially concerns bounties whose corrupted versions are found in the world; but it can be concluded from Quran that in Paradise there would be numerous bounties, which are much more superior and so extraordinary that they were neither heard nor seen. Nor the human heart had ever imagined them. The Holy Quran says:

"So no soul knows what is hidden for them of that which will refresh the eyes…" (32:17)

The Messenger of Allah (s) said:
"There are such bounties in Paradise that neither the human eye has seen them nor the human heart has imagined."[124]

Bounties of Paradise would come in search of the believer and not that the believer has to go out in search of them. Amirul Momineen ('a) said:

"Tooba is a tree in Paradise; its roots are in the house of the Messenger of Allah (s), and it will have a branch in the house of every believer; whenever a believer desires something, it would be given to him by that branch."[125]

The folks of Paradise would remain in perpetual youth and elegance. Senility, disease, weakness, pain, sorrow, jealousy enmity and worry have no place in Paradise. People of Paradise would enjoy the different types of foods, but would not produce any excrement. They would live in Paradise forever and death will never come to them.

The late Mulla Mohsin Faiz Kashani has mentioned the difference between the bounties of Paradise and the bounties of the world:

Desire of man is under the control of things, which are beyond existence but the matters of Paradise would be under the control of the folks of Paradise. Whatever they desire would be given to them only by wishing for it. The Almighty Allah says in the Holy Quran:

---

[124] Wasailush Shia, Vol. 11, Pg. 476

[125] Biharul Anwar, Vol. 8, Pg. 117

> *"...Therein shall be what their souls yearn after and (wherein) the eyes shall delight..."(43:71)*

Thus whatever they intend would be given to them immediately and not that what is present at that time.[126] Another difference is that the growth of the hereafter is the growth of effulgence, perception, divine proximity, life and appearance; matters of the hereafter are alive and perceptible. As mentioned in traditions, different fruits would tell the folks of Paradise: 'O Wali of Allah, eat me before you are inclined to something else.' And when the believer sits on his throne, it would become extremely elated. And it is mentioned in Quran that:

> *"...As for the next abode, that most surely is the life- did they but know!" (29:64)*[127]

Grades of Paradise

Paradise has different grades and ranks. The bounties of Paradise are also not same for all the people of Paradise. All folks of Paradise are not confined to the same place.

Some are placed in lofty positions and some inhabit the lower grades and some occupy the middle stages.

Amirul Momineen ('a) has said in description of Paradise:

"It has more and higher grades; it has different kinds of abodes and its bounties are never exhausted. Its inhabitants never depart and one who lives therein never becomes aged, its folks never fall in any need."[128]

The Quran says:

---

[126] Usul al-Ma'rif, Pg. 197

[127] Usul al-Ma'rif, Pg. 201

[128] Nahjul Balagha, Sermon 85

"There are (varying) grades with Allah, and Allah sees what they do." (3:163)

And it says:

"The holders back from among the believers, not having any injury, and those who strive hard in Allah's way with their property and their persons are not equal; Allah has made the strivers with their property and their persons to excel the holders back a (high) degree, and to each (class) Allah has promised good; and Allah shall grant to the strivers above the holders back a mighty reward." (4:95)

And also says:

"Allah will exalt those of you who believe, and those who are given knowledge, in high degrees; and Allah is Aware of what you do." (58:11)

Also it says:

"And for all are degrees according to what they did, and that He may pay them back fully their deeds and they shall not be wronged." (46:19)

The loftiest stage of Paradise is Rizwan; the Holy Quran says:

> *"..And best of all is Allah's goodly pleasure- that is the grand achievement." (9:72)*

Therefore all the believers would go to Paradise and enjoy the bounties of Paradise; but the abode of Paradise is not same for them all, neither the bounties that they would enjoy. On the contrary there are so many differences between them that our limited intellect cannot understand them all. It is possible that these differences are due to the following reasons:

One: How much divine recognition they have and what are their religious beliefs.

Two: Their mental faculties and potential in observing moral values;

Three: How particular they are in performing their religious duties.

Four: Quantum of piety, refraining from evil traits and abstaining from sins.

Although the people of Paradise would get whatever they intend or wish for, immediately:

> *"...Therein shall be what their souls yearn after and (wherein) the eyes shall delight..."(43:71)*

But the desires of all the people are not same; on the contrary they are dependant on their cognition and faith.

Access to Paradise and enjoying its bounties

Paradise is earned in this same world through faith and correct beliefs, good ethics and deeds and through keeping away from sins and it would become clear in the world of the hereafter. Paradise and its bounties are as a result of the deeds of the world; on the contrary they would be the deeds themselves.

Imam Ja'far Sadiq ('a) said:

"Allah, the exalted and the blessed said: My true servants, enjoy the bounties of My worship in this world, as you will enjoy the same in the world of the hereafter."[129]

The Messenger of Allah (s) said:

"In Paradise there are transparent palaces of glass, which would be occupied by those from my nation, who speak nicely with others, who feed the poor, greet aloud and during the night when people sleep, they are occupied in prayers."[130]

Imam Sajjad ('a) said:

"Be blessed through reciting and acting on the Holy Quran. Indeed the Almighty Allah has created Paradise with bricks of gold and silver. Its mortar is musk; its sand is saffron and emeralds its pebbles. He has made the stages of Paradise as numerous as the verses of Quran. One who recited the Quran in the world (and acted on it) on Judgment Day he would be told: Recite and continue to climb and anyone who enters Paradise would not be higher than him, except the prophets and the truthful ones."[131]

The Messenger of Allah (s) said:

"When on the night of ascension I entered Paradise, I beheld a white plain where a number of angels were building palaces of gold and silver bricks. Now they plied their work, and then they stood idle. I asked them why their labors were interrupted. They replied, "We wait to be paid for our labors." "What payments?" I asked. They answered, "The recital on earth by believers of such ascriptions as: Glory be to Allah, and praise be to Allah, and there is no god except Allah, and Allah is the

---

[129] Biharul Anwar, Vol. 8, Pg. 155

[130] Biharul Anwar, Vol. 8, Pg. 119

[131] Biharul Anwar, Vol. 8, Pg. 133

greatest. Whenever they pronounce these ascriptions, we build; but when they cease, our work also ceases."[132]

The Messenger of Allah (s) also said:

"Generosity is a tree of the trees of Paradise, with branches hanging in the world; one who is generous is taken hold by one of those branches and taken to Paradise. And miserliness is a tree from the trees of Hell; it has branches in the world; thus one who is miserly takes up one of its branches and enters Hell."[133]

Quran says:

> **"And obey Allah and the Apostle, that you may be shown mercy. And hasten to forgiveness from your Lord; and a Garden, the extensiveness of which is (as) the heavens and the earth, it is prepared for those who guard (against evil). Those who spend (benevolently) in ease as well as in straitness, and those who restrain (their) anger and pardon men; and Allah loves the doers of good (to others). And those who when they commit an indecency or do injustice to their souls remember Allah and ask forgiveness for their faults- and who forgives the faults but Allah, and (who) do not knowingly persist in what they have done. (As for) these- their reward is forgiveness from their Lord, and gardens beneath which rivers flow, to abide in them, and excellent is the reward of the laborers." (3:132-136)**

That which is mentioned here was about the perfect Paradise, but as for the Paradise of morals, good qualities and the Paradise of meeting the Lord; it is another thing, to explain which is beyond the aim of this

---

[132] Biharul Anwar, Vol. 8, Pg. 123

[133] Biharul Anwar, Vol. 8, Pg. 171

brief treatise.

Our final statement is: Praise be to Allah, Lord of the worlds. O Allah pity my old age, the termination of my days, the approach of my death and my feebleness, my poverty and the scarcity of resources! Pity me when my trace disappears from the world, my memory is wined off from among the creatures and I be one who is forgotten! My Lord, pity me at my resurrection and my rising (from the grave). On that day, let my place be with Your friends, my exit among Your friends and my dwelling in Your neighborhood, O Lord, of the Worlds! O my God, discontinue Your goodness in my life and do not cut off Your favors on me at my death O the most merciful of the merciful ones.

Bibliography

The Holy Quran

Nahjul Balagha

Majlisi, Allamah Muhammad Baqir, Biharul Anwar, Daar Ahya Turath, Beirut 1403 A.H.

Kulaini, Muhammad bin Yaqoob, Usul al-Kafi, Darul Kutub al-Islamiya, Tehran, 1388 A.H.

Sadruddin Shirazi (Mulla Sadra) Muhammad bin Ibrahim, Al-Asfar al-Arba, Nashr Mustafawi, Qom, [Undated]

Sadruddin Shirazi (Mulla Sadra) Muhammad bin Ibrahim, Risala Tasawwur wa Tasdeeq, Nashr Maula, Tehran [Undated]

Maad az Deedgah Imam Khomeini

Faiz Kashani, Mulla Mohsin, Ilmul Yaqeen

Hurre Amili, Shaykh Muhammad bin Hasan, Wasailush Shia, Mausisa Aale Bayt, Qom, 1407 A.H.

Suyuti, Jalaluddin, Ad-Durre Manthur, Darul Fikr, Beirut 1993 A.D.

Ibne Sina, Husain bin Abdullah, Al-Isharaat wa Tanbihaat, Matba Haidariya, Tehran, 1378 A.H

Epilogue

The Holy Quran has stressed the subject of resurrection more than all the other heavenly scripture and has mentioned it continuously in a large number of verses, from the beginning to the end. This work has studies the various aspects of resurrection from the viewpoint of the Holy Quran discussing in an easy and a fluent style, topics such as the soul, grave, Purgatory, Judgment Day, scroll of deeds, intercession, Siraat Bridge and Paradise and Hell.

This book is part of ideological collection of "The Youth and Beliefs" with topics such as: Knowing God, Resurrection, Prophethood and the Prophet of Islam, Introduction to Islam, Rights and duties of Women, Imamate and the Imams, Youth and Spouse Selection. All these volumes are written by Ayatullah Ibrahim Amini, who has succeeded to author this collection based on years of delving into religious texts and sources, constant contact with the young generation and pondering over ideological and educational issues.

www.ingramcontent.com/pod-product-compliance
Lightning Source LLC
LaVergne TN
LVHW041947070526
838199LV00051BA/2940